THE MAJESTY OF

MUGHAL DECORATION

THE MAJESTY OF
MUGHAL DECORATION
THE ART AND ARCHITECTURE OF ISLAMIC INDIA

GEORGE MICHELL

RESEARCH BY MUMTAZ CURRIM

WITH OVER **300** COLOR ILLUSTRATIONS

Thames & Hudson

First published in 2007 in hardcover in the United States of America by
Thames & Hudson Inc., 500 Fifth Avenue, New York, New York 10110

thamesandhudsonusa.com

Original edition © 2007 India Book House
Text © 2007 George Michell

Library of Congress Catalog Card Number 2007901132

ISBN 978-0-500-51377-4

Printed and bound in China

CONTENTS

INTRODUCTION

THEMES

DOCUMENTATION

*I*NTRODUCTION

THE MUGHALS AS PATRONS

Mughal style was not the invention of any single artist, nor indeed of any particular group of artists; rather, it was the conscious creation of a line of rulers that encouraged, supervised and financed generations of architects, calligraphers, painters, weavers and metalworkers over a period of more than 250 years. The result is an aesthetic that is characterized by subtlety, delicacy and elegance, while at the same time capable of robust expression and confidence. Drawing on the arts of the wider Islamic world, yet firmly rooted in Indian traditions, Mughal style permeated every aspect of the lives of the Mughal emperors, their nobles and members of their private households. It influenced their manners and courtly etiquette; the dishes they used and the wine cups they drank from; their rich apparel and gorgeous jewelry; the opulent interiors of their palaces, covered in magnificent carpets and hung with brocades; the majestic monuments that proclaimed their wealth and might. As if excellence were not enough, each emperor aspired to a greater or lesser degree to perfection itself.

Of all Indian rulers it is the Mughals who most truly deserve the title of Padshahs, Emperors. Supremely successful as commanders of the largest and most disciplined army the country had ever seen, the Mughals brought a large proportion of the Indian subcontinent under their control from the middle of the 16th century onwards. At the height of their power in the 17th century the Mughals were masters of the whole of Hindustan, as northern India was then known, from Kabul beyond the Hindu Kush range in Afghanistan in the far north-west to Bengal in the east where the Ganga and Brahmaputra Rivers converge. To the south, the Mughal empire extended well into the Indian peninsula, though never entirely to the extreme tip. Substantial revenues from these far-ranging domains financed the military campaigns of the Mughals, as well as their grandiose building schemes and *karkhanas*, or imperial workshops, which employed large numbers of expert artists, artisans and craftsmen. The unrivalled series of superbly constructed and decorated monuments that survive from their era, together with the exquisite miniature paintings, woven carpets, inlaid metal objects and carved jades manufactured in their ateliers testify to the sponsorship of successive Mughal emperors. By the time the Mughal empire had finally collapsed in the 19th century, the magnificent architecture and art that they had created in earlier times had exercised an enduring influence on the whole country.

At the outset we must recognize the remarkable unity of the visual world created by the Mughals. The buildings and art objects that they created are imbued with an artistic harmony that surpassed the ordinary limitations of scale and material. Almost exactly the same decorative themes are found in architecture and the fine arts, whether it be a

Shah Jahan, seated on the celebrated Peacock Throne within the public audience hall of his palace at Shahjahanabad in Delhi, accompanied by his sons and nobles. The emperor is decked in gorgeous jewels, and his head is encircled by a golden halo, a motif suggesting divine status, borrowed from Christian iconotaph. In front, on a stand, is a globe symbolizing the emperor's universal authority.
CATALOGUE 7

PAGE 2 Relief panel of an iris with other flowers in a vase, Taj Mahal, Agra.

PAGES 4—5 Facade with ornamental lobed arch, Moti Masjid, Red Fort, Delhi.

PAGES 6—7 *Pietra dura* frieze of poppies and lilies on the upper cenotaph of Shah Jahan, Taj Mahal.

11

monumental gateway of red sandstone, a paper page painted with delicate watercolour, or a woven silken hanging. In this way a unified visual setting was created, in which the emperors and their family members, courtiers and commanders conducted their everyday lives. The unmatched quality of workmanship with which this setting was realized ensured that this style never degenerated into deadening repetition. The exquisitely decorated palaces and mosques, tented camps and pleasure gardens, let alone miniature paintings, textiles and inlaid metal vessels, are all expressions of a genuine delight in the creation of beauty. That such architectural and artistic manifestations of imperial Mughal taste should conform to a coherent aesthetic, which we here term Mughal style, is evidence of a personal interest in building and the fine arts on the part of the emperors themselves. Indeed, as the chronicles of the era make clear, ruling figures met regularly with architects and artists in their employ to discuss building projects and particular works of art, and to reward the most gifted practitioners, many of whose names are registered in the official court records. In this way the emperors were able to exercise their personal tastes and preferences.

BABUR & HUMAYUN

The first of the Mughal line, Babur, was a figure of outstanding aesthetic sensibility. His memoirs, the *Babur Nama*, written in the Chaghatai Turkish language of his Central Asian ancestors, reveal an irrepressible delight in the natural world, as well as in poetry, wine and companionship. However, in his last years Babur was mainly occupied with establishing a Mughal presence in a foreign country. Having conquered Hindustan after his success over Ibrahim Lodi, ruler of the Delhi kingdom, at the legendary battle of Panipat in 1526, Babur ruled for a mere four years before dying in 1530. But in this brief period he established a garden resort at Dholpur in central India where he attempted to recapture the delights of the valley of Ferghana, the Mughal homeland in what is now Uzbekistan.

On Babur's death his son Humayun inherited the structure of a substantial and already wealthy kingdom. But it was not long before he was challenged by Sher Shah Suri, a powerful Afghan commander with a wide following in Hindustan. In 1538 Sher Shah compelled Humayun to flee India. Over the next 15 years Humayun led a wandering life as a prince in search of a lost kingdom. For a time he sought refuge in Tabriz at the court of Shah Tahmasp, the Safavid ruler of Persia, who offered sympathy and support. It is proof of Humayun's charismatic personality that he eventually gathered around him a band of loyal followers, who then accompanied him on his return to India. Upon vanquishing Sher Khan, Sher Shah Sultan's son, in 1555, Humayun once again established the Mughal presence in Hindustan, this time on a permanent basis. Significantly, in his retinue were architects, painters, weavers and other artisans that he had recruited in Persia and Afghanistan, trained in the finest Safavid traditions. These craftsmen formed the core of the workshops that were developed by his son Akbar, who unexpectedly assumed the Mughal throne in 1556 at the tender age of 14, when Humayun fell accidentally to his death in Delhi's Purana Qila, barely one year after returning to India.

AKBAR

With Akbar we are in the presence of a truly extraordinary personality who may be considered the most energetic and innovative of all Mughal imperial patrons. Akbar's first great building project was the tomb of his father, erected in 1564–71 on the bank of the Yamuna River in Delhi, partly financed by Haji Begum, Humayun's widow. However, Humayun's tomb represents only the beginning of Akbar's involvement with monumental architecture. After leading the Mughal forces in a number of triumphant military expeditions, even when still a teenager, Akbar embarked upon a series of large-scale constructional projects, first at Agra, further downstream on the Yamuna, and then at Lahore in Punjab, where he was mostly based at the end of his eventful, 49-year-long reign. At both these centres Akbar raised substantial fortified citadels from where he ruled over his rapidly increasing territories, holding court in imposing ceremonial halls, and enjoying more private pleasures in the adjacent apartments, terraces and gardens that he laid out for himself and his different queens.

The most remarkable of Akbar's building ventures, and the one that still stands most completely, is, however, Fatehpur Sikri, the red sandstone city located a short distance west of Agra. Akbar founded this city in fulfillment of a vow that he had made to Shaykh Salim Chishti, the Sufi saint who lived here and who had predicted the birth of a son. In 1569 a son was born here and named Salim after the saint himself. The fanciful designs of the various reception halls and residential apartments of the palace complex that he erected at Fatehpur Sikri over some 15 years from 1569 onwards provide a fascinating architectural overview of the different regions of India that Akbar had by this time brought under his control. Having annexed Gujarat in western India in 1573, he promptly imported expert craftsmen from this province to work at Fatehpur Sikri. Turning to Rajasthan, Akbar embarked upon a policy of treaties and alliances. Accordingly, he married the daughter of Raja Bharmal of Amber in 1562, and it was this princess who bore him Prince Salim. The so-called palace of Jodh Bai at Fatehpur Sikri, the residence of Akbar's Rajput wife and female retinue, imitates a typical Rajasthani palace. Akbar was a devout Muslim and each of his fortified headquarters was provided with a monumental Jami mosque for assembling his courtiers, military officers and soldiers. The largest of these places of prayer is the Jami mosque at Fatehpur Sikri, completed in 1575. In its courtyard Akbar erected an exquisite marble tomb for Salim Chishti after the saint died in 1581. Towards the end of his reign Akbar began work on his own mausoleum at Sikandra on the outskirts of Agra, but this project remained unfinished at his death in 1605.

Whether Akbar was illiterate or dyslexic as is sometimes thought has never been definitely established, but there is no doubt that he had difficulty reading; perhaps for this reason he was particularly attracted to all things visual. On attaining the Mughal throne, Akbar immediately set up a *kitabkhana*, a library with an attendant workshop which produced paintings and calligraphic and illuminated manuscripts. This came under the able direction of 'Abd as-Samad, one of the Persian painters who had been brought to India by Humayun. More specialists were soon required and indigenous talent was recruited and trained. It was this mingling of Persian and Indian experts that led to the creation of a genuine Mughal pictorial style. Illustrated books were a favourite with Akbar. One of the first and most ambitious works that he commissioned was the *Hamza Nama*, the adventures of a legendary hero, which appeared in 10 volumes, each supplied with 140 pictures. The *kitabkhana* was occupied with this assignment for more than 15 years, beginning in 1562. During the 1580s and 1590s the workshop was taken up with producing illustrated historical works that included Akbar's own biography, the *Akbar Nama*, authored by his trusted confidant and adviser, Abu'l Fazl, and a Persian translation of the *Babur Nama*, the autobiography of his grandfather.

At the same time Akbar ordered fresh versions of Persian literary classics such as the *Gulistan* of Sa'di and *Khamsa* of Nizami, which were also richly embellished with miniatures. Akbar's taste extended also to the indigenous literature of India, and he became fascinated with Hindu mythology, commissioning Persian translations of the popular *Ramayana* and *Mahabharata* epics that were similarly supplied with illustrations. Akbar had early on in his reign developed an interest in Christianity, welcoming Catholic missionaries from the Portuguese colony at Goa to his court. From the mid-1580s onwards he instructed his atelier to make copies of the Biblical engravings that these visitors brought with them to Agra and Lahore.

The activities of Akbar's workshops were by no means restricted to painting as confirmed by the splendid carpets produced in Agra, Fatehpur Sikri and Lahore, where special ateliers, known as *karkhanas*, were set up with imported weavers to train local craftsmen. The superb floral and animal patterns of these carpets are in the finest Persian tradition; so, too, the designs of the exquisitely woven cotton and silk costumes worn at Akbar's court. Akbar also employed metalworkers to manufacture ceremonial weapons and arms that were in themselves works of art. An engraved copper bowl that survives from his era is decorated with the scenes of hunting and drinking that must have been favourite pastimes of the emperor and his companions. Sadly, the last years of Akbar's reign were marred by disappointments, especially disagreements with Salim, who rebelled against his father. Father and son were eventually reconciled in 1604, one year before Akbar died, after which Salim inherited the Mughal throne under the name Jahangir.

This lifelike portrait of a peregrine falcon is typical of the miniatures commissioned by Jahangir, who took a particular interest in the natural world. Among the artists in his employ who specialized in this type of painting, no doubt under the influence of European nature studies, was Mansur, whose signature appears above the bird. The painting is mounted on a floral border of later date. CATALOGUE 11

JAHANGIR

Like Akbar, Jahangir had a true appreciation of literature and was steeped in the delights of the Persian classics; he was, however, highly educated and even exhibited skills as a talented calligrapher. Jahangir inherited Akbar's taste for architecture, completing his father's tomb at Sikandra by adding a magnificently decorated entrance gateway; he also extended the palace structures within the forts at Agra and Lahore. But perhaps his greatest love was for garden resorts; in 1620 he laid out Shalimar Bagh on the bank of the picturesque Dal Lake in Kashmir. That gardens formed part of Jahangir's overall fascination with nature is evident from the pictorial studies of flowers, animals and birds that were produced in his *kitabkhana*. Jahangir seems to have taken more delight in these naturalistic illustrations than those that accompanied epic stories or royal biographies. From Jahangir's reign we also have a number of lifelike portraits of courtly personalities that reveal another aspect of the emperor's interest in realism. Like Akbar, Jahangir too was attracted to European subjects, and many reproductions of Portuguese figures and Biblical scenes were made at his direct orders. These paintings reveal the emperor's refined aesthetic tastes, as do the exquisite velvets and carved jades assigned to his era. However, while Jahangir was able to satisfy his artistic needs by surrounding himself with beautiful objects, he seems also to have developed other less worthwhile habits, succumbing to opium in the later years of his reign. It was under these circumstances that the affairs of state were increasingly taken over by his queen Nur Jahan. An outstanding personality and capable administrator, Nur Jahan did not hesitate to act as a patron in her own right, laying out an exquisite garden tomb for her father Itimad-ad Daula on the left bank of the Yamuna at Agra in 1626–28, and building her own mausoleum in Lahore in 1645.

SHAH JAHAN

In the last years of Jahangir's life control of the empire deteriorated, encouraging competition between his three sons. However, at the death of the emperor in 1628 it was his second son, Khurram, who eliminated his rival brothers and, assuming the title of Shah Jahan, seized the Mughal throne. Under Shah Jahan's expert rule the empire continued to expand. Mughal rule in the Kabul valley of Afghanistan and the riverine delta of Bengal at the other end of Hindustan was firmly established once and for all. But it was in the Deccan that the Mughal armies made their greatest advance, threatening and eventually overwhelming the kingdoms of Ahmadnagar, Bijapur and Golconda. Not to be outdone by his father and grandfather, Shah Jahan rapidly established himself as a great builder. Since Jahangir had died erecting his own tomb, one of the first tasks that Shah Jahan set himself was the construction of a mausoleum for his father at Shahdara on the outskirts of Lahore. Before it was finished in 1638 he had already begun work on the Taj Mahal at Agra, which he raised in memory of his beloved wife Mumtaz Mahal, who had sadly died early on in his reign in 1631. Under construction up to 1643, the Taj Mahal is the outstanding masterpiece of Mughal architecture, unmatched for its grandeur of conception, perfect proportions and sumptuous ornamentation. Little wonder that it has earned for Shah Jahan a place among the greatest patrons of world art. That such an ambitious monument could successfully be completed is a testament to the human and financial resources that the emperor willingly made available, and the personal attention that he gave to the project, visiting the site whenever possible.

The Taj Mahal was by no means Shah Jahan's only significant architectural endeavour. In 1639 he conceived the idea of building a new walled city at Delhi, named after himself as Shahjahanabad. Over a period of almost 10 years this city was laid out on the bank of the Yamuna, only a short distance from the tomb of his great-grandfather Humayun. The citadel of Shahjahanabad was provided with massive ramparts and defensive gateways that protected the palace complex within. A covered bazaar inside the walls led to a sequence of reception halls, apartments and pleasure gardens. A magnificent Jami mosque with monumental portals was raised just outside. At the same time Shah Jahan ordered similar palace structures to be added to the older Mughal fortresses at Agra and Lahore. Such intense building activity, surpassing that of his predecessors and never equalled by his successors, is evidence that Shah Jahan regarded architecture as a means of expressing the might of the Mughal empire. Nor were these the only major projects of his era; in 1648 his daughter Jahanara ordered a new Jami to be erected in Agra. Shah Jahan also inspired several of his officers to act as patrons. Among them was Wazir Khan, governor of Punjab, who in 1634 built a mosque, with brilliantly coloured tiles that still bear its patron's name, tucked away in the old city of Lahore.

Under Shah Jahan painting was also harnessed to the glorification of the imperial image. The most important events in the life of the emperor were illustrated in the superbly finished miniatures of the *Padshah Nama* that recorded the minute details of courtly receptions, visitations, feasts and battles. These history paintings are crammed with realistic details of palace interiors, cities, fortresses and landscapes. They were supplemented by a profusion of portraits of Shah Jahan himself and his various courtiers and commanders that issued forth from the imperial workshops. Such a concern with formal representation by no means signalled a lack of interest in more private pursuits on the part of the emperor. Pages of Persian calligraphy and studies of saintly men demonstrate the emperor's sincere interest in literature and religion. The imperial taste also extended to the appreciation of beautiful objects, exquisite jewelry, carved jade cups and gilded velvet hangings that survive from the era. Even Shah Jahan's weapons were transformed into works of art, judging from the daggers and swords inlaid with jewels in gold settings. The magnificent Ming period, blue and white dishes imported from China, inscribed with Shah Jahan's name, confirm that this emperor was also an inveterate collector of exotic art objects.

DARA SHIKOH & AURANGZEB

Shah Jahan's sons inherited their father's love of the arts, none more so than the eldest, Dara Shikoh. While governor of Allahabad in the 1640s, this prince set up an independent *karkhana* that produced elegant portraits of plants and animals, somewhat in the style of his grandfather Jahangir. Not unlike his great-grandfather Akbar, Dara Shikoh was deeply interested in indigenous Indian culture, studying Sanskrit, and collaborating with the Brahmin scholars of Banaras on a Persian translation of the Upanishads, the ancient Indian spiritual treatises. Though it was Dara Shikoh who was most favoured by Shah Jahan to succeed to the Mughal throne, his younger brothers, especially Shah Shuja, Aurangzeb and Murad Baksh, were also thirsty for power. War broke out between them in 1657, and after a series of skirmishes it was Aurangzeb who emerged victor. Vanquishing and putting to death his siblings, and imprisoning his father within the confines of Agra fort, Aurangzeb seized the Mughal throne in 1658. The reign of this emperor, the sixth in the Mughal line, was to be exactly as long as Akbar's, lasting 49 years. It was, however, not nearly so eventful from the point of view of patronage of architecture and the fine arts. This was probably because a major part of Aurangzeb's career was taken up with campaigning in the Deccan, at first as a conqueror storming the citadels of Golconda and Bijapur in 1666–67, then as the founder of a new capital, named after him as Aurangabad. This city served as the second Mughal headquarters after Delhi up until his death in 1707. Aurangzeb's rule in the Deccan, however, was repeatedly challenged by Shivaji, the Maratha warrior chief and founder of the Hindu military confederacy that was to emerge as a major power in India during the course of the 18th century.

Once established on the throne Aurangzeb undertook several grandiose architectural schemes, the most impressive of which was the Badshahi mosque at Lahore, the largest of all Mughal religious structures, as well as lesser mosques at Mathura, Banaras and Aurangabad. Aurangzeb is also credited with founding the *madrasa* of Ghazi al-Din Khan in Delhi, and a series of well-provisioned caravanserais on the highways linking the Mughal capitals of Hindustan. The tomb that Aurangzeb built in 1661 for his queen Rabia Daurani on the outskirts of Aurangabad, known as the Bibi-ka Maqbara, was also partly the work of his son Azam Shah, when serving as commander in the Deccan.

While Aurangzeb is supposed to have been less committed to the fine arts than his predecessors, there is no shortage of miniature paintings assigned to his reign. Admittedly, many of these are conventional portraits of the emperor himself and his nobles, but there are also scenes with women, musicians and poets to suggest that life at Aurangzeb's court was by no means lacking in pleasurable diversions. *Karkhanas* at the different imperial centres, including the Deccan cities that had recently been absorbed into the Mughal domains, were kept busy fulfilling orders for carpets and costly textiles, weapons with carved hilts, and metallic ewers and basins inlaid with gold and silver. In the end, however, religion prevailed over imperial glory. Aurangzeb ordered that he should be buried not in an imposing garden mausoleum like his predecessors, but in a simple open-air grave at Khuldabad, near Aurangabad, within the shrine complex of a Chishti saint whose teachings he revered.

THE LATER MUGHALS

In the years after Aurangzeb's death the Mughal empire experienced an irreversible decline, due partly to the relentless assaults by the Maratha troops under their Scindia and Holkar commanders, who pushed ever northwards into the Mughal heartland of Hindustan. Then came the blow of 1739 when Nadir Shah of Persia audaciously raided Delhi, carrying away the greater portion of the Mughal armoury and treasury, including the celebrated Peacock Throne. As the 18th century progressed, many Mughal governors broke away from Delhi to found their own independent kingdoms. In this way the province of Awadh in eastern Hindustan became the headquarters of an independent line of nawabs, while the lucrative Deccan provinces were transformed into the Hyderabad kingdom, under the fabulously wealthy Nizams. In spite of this inevitable erosion of the Mughal empire and its fortunes, building activity in Delhi continued, especially under various nobles. Raushan al-Daula Zafar Khan, Prime Minister of Muhammad Shah who ruled from 1719 to 1748, for instance, was responsible for several mosques that were finer than any sponsored by the emperor himself. Safdar Jang, governor of Awadh under Muhammad Shah's successor, Ahmad Shah, built for himself an elegant marble-domed tomb on the outskirts of Delhi in 1754. Mughal queens at this time also acted as patrons. Among them was Qudsiya Begum, mother of Ahmad Shah, who commissioned a lavish garden palace within the walls of Shahjahanabad. This revival of Delhi's architecture came to an abrupt end with the uprising of 1857, after which the British occupied the city, imprisoning Bahadur Shah Zafar II, the last of the illustrious Mughal line.

Painting and the other arts in these times continued to be produced at the imperial *karkhanas* and at other centres, as orders were forthcoming from the nobility and lesser members of the royal family. The 18th century, in fact, witnessed an efflorescence in miniature painting and the decorative arts. Costumes and textiles in silk and wool, water vessels and *huqqa* bowls of metal inlaid with gold and silver, and turban ornaments and weapons encrusted with diamonds, rubies and enamels were all executed in the finest Mughal manner. If the glory of the empire was waning, with the later emperors presiding over a rapidly diminishing territory, there was no perceptible decline in the production of art objects of the highest quality. To the contrary, Mughal style continued to flourish in the provincial courts of India that emerged during the course of the 18th century. It even survived after the last Mughal emperor had died in exile in Burma in 1862.

FOLLOWING PAGES At the heart of Akbar's palace city of Fatehpur Sikri is a huge red sandstone courtyard surrounded by fanciful structures, reception halls and water bodies. The Panch Mahal at left, for members of the harem, consists of five-pillared storeys, diminishing in size to a single large *chhatri*. The small square building at centre is the Diwan-i Khass, Akbar's hall of private audience, noted for its massive central pillar inside.

ARTISTIC SOURCES & INFLUENCES

The splendour and refinement of Mughal style are unmistakable; so too its artistic individuality. Rarely is there any difficulty in recognizing that a building or work of art belongs to the Mughal era. Whether expressed in architecture, miniature painting or the decorative arts, Mughal style has a quality that distinguishes it from contemporary art traditions in other parts of the Islamic world, such as that of Safavid Persia or Ottoman Turkey, let alone the pre-Mughal traditions of India itself. The outstanding aesthetic distinctiveness of Mughal style is perhaps best explained in terms of the diverse sources that it draws upon, and which it synthesizes in the most brilliant manner possible.

THE HERITAGE OF CENTRAL ASIA

The Mughals were ethnic Turks of Mongol origin hailing from Central Asia. Even after several generations of continuous occupation of India and intermarriage with local Hindu royal families, the Mughals always retained a sense of their Central Asian identity, in spite of the fact that they were never able to regain possession of their country of origin. It was perhaps this sense of a lost homeland that underpinned their preference for architectural projects and art objects of Central Asian form and design, and their ongoing mission to attract to their court military, literary and religious figures, as well as master masons and craftsmen from Uzbekistan and Afghanistan.

Mughal style is dominated by the artistic accomplishments of Timur and Shahrukh, the illustrious 15th-century ancestors of the Mughal line. The Mughal emperors never forgot the great mosques, tombs and palaces built by these figures in Samarkand and Herat, even though it was only Babur who had the opportunity of actually visiting these for himself. The earliest Mughal buildings on Indian soil may be interpreted as re-creations of Timurid models, as seen in the use of facades with formal arched portals, and domes with bulbous profiles raised on cylindrical drums. The preference for geometric designs and elegant arabesque motifs also harks back to Timurid usage. However, instead of cloaking brick structures with vividly coloured ceramic tiles, as the Timurids had done in Samarkand and Herat, the Mughals adapted rapidly to Indian conditions, creating polychrome effects out of locally available, different coloured stones. They also presented a novel synthesis of two, previously unlinked architectural ideas: the *char-bagh* or four-square paradise garden of Persian origin, and the dynastic tomb, both of which had been utilized by Timur himself, though never together in a single complex. Humayun's mausoleum in Delhi stands in the middle of a formally planned garden divided into squares. But unlike its Timurid antecedents it presents four identical, outward facing arched portals.

This exquisitely rendered *shamsa*, or sunburst rosette, presents an outer ring of 16 lobed cartouches filled with intricate arabesque ornament on gold and blue backgrounds. The cartouches encircle a *tughra*, a medallion inscribed with the names and titles of Shah Jahan. Painted in the finest Central Asian manner of the 15th century, this illumination serves as a spectacular opener for an album of miniatures collected by the emperor himself. CATALOGUE 1

In the fine arts of the Mughal period there is a parallel concern with continuing the Timurid aesthetic. Not only did the Mughals bring with them to India illuminated manuscripts, silk carpets, jade bowls and even Chinese ceramic dishes that had once belonged to their Timurid forebears, they then ordered that such works be imitated at their imperial *kitabkhanas* and *karkhanas*. Little wonder that the shapes and motifs that pervade so many of the decorative objects fashioned for the Mughal emperors were Timurid in inspiration. Timurid traditions also dominate Mughal decorative design, as can be seen in the fluid arabesque motifs contained in lobed medallions executed in diverse materials and techniques: delicately carved sandstone relief; inset multi-coloured precious stones; woven silk fabric; interlacing gold strips inserted into jade; even minute mother-of-pearl pieces glued onto wood. Calligraphy, whether in Arabic or Persian, is often Timurid in style and presentation, being contained in ornamental bands and lobed cartouches on architectural portals and, in miniature form, painted in ink on paper or engraved onto brass bowls and jade cups. Timurid arabesques of outstanding elegance also serve as frames and even as backgrounds to calligraphy, both in inlaid polychrome stonework and colour tile mosaic on mosque facades, and painted in brilliant gold and blue onto the frontispieces of Korans and anthologies of Persian poetry. The delicately painted *shamsas*, or sunbursts, that frame imperial signatures, with which some collections of miniatures begin, are also of obvious Timurid inspiration.

PERSIAN TRADITIONS

The transmission of Timurid artistic practices that have just been outlined was for the most part accomplished via the expertise of Persian artists who sought employment at the Mughal court, beginning with those painters and craftsmen that Humayun brought with him to India on his triumphant return in 1555. Thereafter there was a steady influx of Persian architects, calligraphers and artists, many of whose names are recorded on Mughal buildings and miniature paintings. Together with Persian nobles, mercenaries, religious figures and literati these immigrants from Iran kept Safavid artistic and intellectual traditions very much alive on Indian soil. Indeed, Mughal patronage of such traditions began more or less at the same time that sponsorship declined in Persia itself towards the middle of the 16th century, when the Safavid ruler Shah Tahmasp dismissed artists and intellectuals from his court at Tabriz. Indeed it is tempting to conclude that Safavid culture found ultimate fulfillment not in its home country but in India. Only in the early 17th century were such artistic traditions revived in Persia itself, under Shah Abbas; by then, however, the Safavid style was firmly established at the Mughal court.

Mughal architecture inherits the full complement of Safavid ornamental devices, best seen in the smoothly pointed arches and complex stalactite vaults animated with elegant arabesque motifs. The flowering plants, blossoms in fanciful vases, and intertwined cypresses and plant motifs of Mughal decoration are typical expressions of Safavid taste; so too the arched niches framing outlines of vases with narrow necks. That such obviously Persian designs were realized in stone worked in shallow relief, polychrome inlays or perforated *jali* screens is evidence of the ability of architects working in India, even if of actual Persian origin, to adapt these imported themes to locally available materials and long established, constructional techniques. The love of formally planned gardens, invariably of the *char-bagh* type, divided into four squares and cooled by water flowing in channels, chutes and fountains, may also be traced to Persia. Yet the fact remains that the largest, most elaborate and best preserved Persian-style gardens of all are those laid out by the Mughal emperors in their palaces in Delhi and Agra and their hill resorts in Kashmir. The Shalimar garden outside the Mughal capital at Lahore, for example, even combines two *char-baghs* at different levels, linked by an ornamental cascade of water flowing through a pleasure pavilion.

The Mughal imperial ateliers were dominated by Persian practice. The first *kitabkhana*, where new works of art were produced, was established under the direction of 'Abd as-Samad and Mir Sayyid Ali, two painters who had previously worked for Shah Tahmasp, but who found themselves unemployed when the Safavid rulers lost interest in the arts. As the years passed these renowned artists were joined by other émigré Persian masters. Much encouraged by Akbar and Jahangir, they undertook the training of local talents in order to expand the production of miniature paintings. Calligraphers, illuminators, weavers, metalworkers and other specialists trained in Safavid styles and techniques must also have been employed at the imperial workshops, judging by the exquisitely finished manuscript illustrations and tooled leather bindings, sumptuous woven carpets and velvets, and embossed silver and brass vessels that were created at this time.

Accompanying the production of such obviously Persian-inspired works of art was a sustained love of Persian language and literature. Akbar, Jahangir and Shah Jahan all commissioned their own copies of classic Persian epics, such as the *Hamza Nama* and *Shah Nama*, as well as collections of romantic tales by Persian luminaries, like Sa'di, Hafiz, Nizami and Anwari. Akbar set the precedent since he took particular delight in the vividly toned illustrations that accompanied such texts. Jahangir prided himself on being able to recognize the hands of the different painters employed in his atelier. Such imperial sensitivities to the visual world influenced the manufacture of paintings, carpets and other works of art of the highest quality. The dominance of Persian cultural traditions at the Mughal court, however, was accompanied by the intrusion of artistic forms and techniques promoted by indigenous exponents. Such local artists were responsible for modifying the Safavid manner so as to create a novel idiom that was uniquely Indian. It is this fusion of imported and local traditions that underscores the genesis and development of Mughal style, contributing to its brilliance and vitality.

THE INDIAN CONTRIBUTION

As the Mughal empire expanded to the extremities of northern India and into the peninsular to the south it encompassed an ever-widening territory that incorporated a broad range of regional building forms and practices. These were absorbed into an architectural manner that rapidly took on the aesthetic and technical dimensions of a genuinely imperial style. From Gujarat and Rajasthan in the west came columned halls and *jharokas*, or elaborate balconies, as well as *chhajjas*, or angled overhangs, domes created out of corbelled rings of cut stone blocks, and perforated stone screens known as *jalis*. Rooftop pavilions with corbelled domes, called *chhatris*, derived from central India and Rajasthan, while Bengal in the east contributed the *bangla* pavilion with its pronounced curving ridge and cornices. Typically Indian in origin and usage, these elements were all adopted by the Mughals for their own civic and religious monuments. The *jharoka*, in particular, came to serve as a throne or balcony for the emperors to display themselves on ceremonial occasions. That all these components, not to mention the imported Central Asian and Persian building forms that have already been noticed, were realized in red sandstone and/or white marble only serves to demonstrate that Mughal architecture was inescapably the product of Indian craftsmen working in local materials, even if Persian trained masters were sometimes in charge. With the exception of monuments in and around Lahore, the colour tilework that characterizes the brick built monuments of buildings in Central Asia and Persia was for the most part replaced by stone, decorated either with delicate relief carvings or polychrome inlays. Painted and relief plasterwork, such as that commonly employed in Persian architecture, found only limited usage in India because its fragile nature was ill-suited to the country's harsh climatic conditions.

Miniature painting at the Mughal *kitabkhanas* also evolved under the hands of Indian artists. Among the names that have come down to us from Akbar's period are Miskin, Kesu Das and Basawan, all three Hindus. They were among the many Indian artists whose talents came to influence the development of a Mughal pictorial manner that steadily departed from that of the Timurid and Safavid masters, on which it was originally based. Not only is there the intrusion of obvious indigenous motifs, such as Indian costumes, turbans, facial types and landscape features, there is an overall tendency towards more intense colour schemes delighting in bold tonal contrasts that were totally unknown in Persian art. Even more striking is the tendency towards an overall realism, whether in closely observed portraits of the Mughal emperors and their nobles, or in representations of animals and birds, trees and flowers. This irrepressible delight in the world of nature is by no means restricted to miniature painting; it pervades all aspects of Mughal decorative arts, from woven carpets and engraved metal vessels to relief marble panels and carved jades and ivories. Underscoring this naturalism was the ancient Indian notion that nature in all of its manifestations was a propitious force that must always be acknowledged. How else to

The repeated floral motifs in gleaming silks of this late 17th-century garden carpet derive from the Persian tradition. However, in the hands of weavers employed at one of the Mughal *karkhanas* in Agra or Lahore the flowers take on the naturalism and vivid colours that are typical of Mughal style. In such ways were Persian artistic ideas transformed by Indian craftsmen. CATALOGUE 19

explain, for instance, the appearance of lotus finials on the domes of Mughal mosques and tombs, and Indian flowering plants in the borders of marble panels, miniature paintings and woven sashes and shawls? Vivid compositions crammed with identifiable details of everyday life in the towns, villages and countryside of India also come to illustrate Persian translations of the *Ramayana* and *Bhagavata Purana* that related the exploits of Rama and Krishna.

Though all Mughal emperors promoted the development of artistic skills imported from Safavid Persia to their *karkhanas* in Agra, Fatehpur Sikri and Lahore, they also took trouble to encourage Indian craftsmen working in indigenous materials and techniques, especially those connected with the textile industry. Mughal style encompasses block printed cottons from Ahmedabad in Gujarat, gold threaded textiles from Chanderi in central India, woven woollen shawls from Kashmir, and brilliantly coloured, cotton floor cloths and wall hangings from manufacturing centres on the Coromandel coast of peninsular India, the last produced by a laborious process of dyeing, printing and painting known as *kalamkari*. The wooden furniture inset with mother-of-pearl and ivory pieces manufactured in Gujarat and Sindh on the Arabian Sea coast represents yet another facet of the diverse Indian craft traditions that were to make a contribution to Mughal style.

EUROPEAN INFLUENCE

A crucial component of Mughal style is that inspired by works of European art. These were first introduced to India by the Portuguese missionaries who were invited by Akbar and Jahangir to attend their courts at Fatehpur Sikri and Agra. The Portuguese brought with them copies of the Bible illustrated with copious engravings, with which they hoped to convert the emperors to Christianity. Though ultimately failing in this endeavour, the Portuguese nonetheless succeeded in acquainting the Mughal emperors and their artists with the buildings and pictorial art of Renaissance Europe. Indian architects and painters were fascinated by what must have seemed to them an unfamiliar, exotic visual tradition as evident from the European features that make an appearance in Mughal monuments and miniatures from the end of the 16th century onwards. In time these features were to become essential attributes of Mughal style.

European Renaissance influence in Mughal architecture is detected in the subtle modification of building details, such as columns that assume Italianate, vase-like bases and fluted shafts, and arches with semicircular Neoclassical profiles. Arabesque motifs tend to lose their fluidity and tendency towards the infinite, and become more rounded, confined and geometric, in accordance with Italianate taste. Nowhere is this better seen than in the Taj Mahal, where the spandrels of the arches over the principal portals are filled with Renaissance-inspired curving arcs, some of which even resemble European lyres. And then there is the *pietra dura* work with which all the finest Mughal buildings were decorated, especially during the period of Shah Jahan. That *pietra dura* is an imported technique is apparent from the panels of Italian workmanship that are set into the wall immediately behind Shah Jahan's personal throne in the Diwan-i Amm, or hall of public audience, in the Red Fort in Delhi. Depicting birds and flowers, and even a scene of the Greek god Orpheus playing the lute, these panels are created in mosaics of tightly fitting, different coloured stones set into black marble. Indian craftsmen must have quickly mastered the difficulties of this technique since Shah Jahan's palaces in Agra and Delhi and his cenotaph in the Taj Mahal are enhanced with exquisitely executed, floral, arabesque and calligraphic *pietra dura* designs employing a full range of semiprecious stones inlaid into marble.

Miniatures also register the impact of Renaissance art. Aside from direct copies of Christian compositions produced in the *kitabkhanas*, no doubt at the insistence of the emperors themselves, Mughal painting rapidly absorbed European stylistic characteristics. To begin with there was a newly developed awareness of perspective, in which scenes were furnished with background features executed in softened and subdued tones so as to suggest receding planes of an actual landscape. Human figures developed rounded faces and limbs, emphasized by gentle shading so as to suggest bodies in actual three dimensions; many of these figures were cloaked in billowing draperies derived from the costumes worn by European Madonnas and saints. In this way Mughal pictorial art took on a previously unknown, fresh and vigorous naturalism.

Another facet of this European inspired naturalism is to be seen in the studies of flowers, animals and birds. These Mughal compositions were almost certainly influenced by the European natural history paintings or engravings that found their way to the Mughal courts, though none of the originals have survived in India. As has already been observed, Jahangir was fascinated by such studies of flora and fauna, and the finest examples date from his reign, many of them executed by Mansur, one of the greatest Mughal specialists of this type of painting. The quasi-naturalistic flowers and plants that make an appearance in architectural decoration and the fine arts were in all likelihood modelled on illustrated European herbals that were familiar to Mughal artists. Rows of flowers readily identifiable as the iris, tulip, poppy and lily, even if not always reproduced with botanical accuracy, are carved in shallow relief in sandstone or marble, or recreated in dazzling *pietra dura* mosaics employing lapis lazuli and other brightly coloured, imported stones. Arrays of similar flowers occupy the central fields of imperial carpets, or are woven into the borders of sashes and shawls. They adorn metal trays and bowls with inlaid gold and silver designs. Flowers and leaves also find naturalistic expression in monochrome carved jade and crystal cups and bowls. Even more lifelike are the faithful depictions of animal heads, especially of horses, antelopes, rams and *nilgai*, with which the hard stone hilts of daggers and swords are sometimes sculpted.

BEYOND THE MUGHAL DOMAINS

Mughal style in both architecture and the fine arts was vigorously promoted by Akbar and his successors as the visual idiom of an empire that continued to expand over the next 200 years, until by the end of the 17th century this style had spread to the greater part of the country, extending well into the peninsular. But Mughal style also spread beyond the imperial frontiers, and even survived the eventual dissolution of the empire in the 19th century, by which time it had established itself as *the* style *par excellence* in much of India. The first indications of the dissemination of Mughal style outside the confines of empire may be seen in the Hindu kingdoms of Rajasthan, many of which enjoyed beneficial alliances with the Mughal emperors. It was Akbar who first devised the scheme of marrying the daughters of his Rajput contemporaries, and compelling the Rajput princes to serve in his army. In this way the Rajputs were inducted into Mughal courtly life, where many of them enjoyed successful careers as military commanders and provincial governors in the far-flung territories of the empire, broken by spells in the company of the emperors themselves at the principal Mughal capitals. It is this close exposure to Mughal culture that explains the widespread influence of Mughal style on the architecture and art of Rajasthan.

A leading figure in this regard is Mirza Raja Jai Singh, ruler of the Kachhawaha kingdom in north-eastern Rajasthan from 1621 to 1667, who served under both Shah Jahan and Aurangzeb. His additions to the Kachhawaha palace in Amber are executed in the most refined Mughal manner. The Jai Mandir of the second courtyard is adorned with superb, Mughal styled marble reliefs, inlaid mirror work and perforated geometric screens. The *shish mahal*, or mirror hall, at the upper level of Jai Mandir surpasses in brilliance and complexity the mirror halls of the Mughals themselves! The palace built in 1727 by Maharaja Sawai Jai Singh II at the new Kachhawaha capital of Jaipur is equally Mughal inspired. At the core of this complex is a Mughal-styled Diwan-i Amm where Jai Singh conducted the everyday business of state; its typical lobed arches resemble those of the Mughal audience halls in Agra, Delhi and Lahore.

Nor were the Kachhawahas the only Rajputs to build in the Mughal manner. The Sisodias of Udaipur, for instance, ordered Mughal styled additions to their dynastic residence overlooking Pichola Lake in south-eastern Rajasthan. The island pavilion at Udaipur known as Jag Mandir, built entirely in white marble and roofed with a dome that imitates that of a Mughal tomb, even served as the refuge for Prince Khurram, the future Shah Jahan, after his rebellion against his father Jahangir in 1627–28. Other Rajput palaces with audience halls and pleasure pavilions furnished with Mughal arches and decorative motifs sprang up all over Rajasthan, as may be seen in Jodhpur, Bikaner and Alwar. As with Amber and Udaipur, such influence is explained by the fact that royal figures from these households spent more years in the service of the Mughals than in their own kingdoms.

Aside from architecture, miniature painting, especially portraiture in the formal Mughal manner, became extremely popular with the Rajput maharajas and their nobles, even if tempered by a Rajasthani preference for bright colours, and an overall tendency to avoid naturalistic perspectival effects. Rajput princes even adopted Mughal costumes and weapons, though they always retained their flamboyant Rajasthani turbans, which in turn found favour in Agra and Delhi. Following Mughal precedent, the Persian language was even adopted for administrative and military terms. After Delhi was ruthlessly raided by Nadir Shah, the Mughal emperors no longer had the resources to act as patrons of the arts. This provided an opportunity for the maharajas to employ some of the artists and craftsmen from the Mughal ateliers. This explains how the unmistakable Mughal idiom flowed into many of the miniature paintings, printed textiles and inlaid jade and steel weapons that were produced at the Rajput courts during the 18th century.

This period also witnessed the rise of a number of successor kingdoms in the former Mughal domains, especially those Muslim states ruled by the Nawabs of Awadh based at Faizabad-Lucknow in the mid-Gangetic valley and by the Nizams of Hyderabad in the Deccan. Founded by former provincial governors under Aurangzeb and his successors, both the Lucknow and Hyderabad kingdoms endeavoured to emulate the splendour of the Mughals.

The city of Faizabad, followed by Lucknow, was noted for lavishly appointed palaces built in the grandest possible manner, recalling the splendours of Agra and Delhi, even if influenced by the new fashion for European Neoclassicism. Master artists and craftsmen from the Mughal *karkhanas* were engaged by the nawabs to create textiles, enamelled vessels and jewelled turban pieces that rivalled the finest items produced for the Mughals. Judging from the obvious Mughal manner of the courtly etiquette that they maintained in Hyderabad until the middle of the 20th century, the Nizams and their nobles were equally concerned to maintain cultural links with the Mughals. The palaces that dotted Hyderabad in the 18th and 19th centuries had obviously Mughal-styled features, while the workshops of the city were kept busy producing woven carpets, inlaid metal vessels and jewelled costumes in the best Mughal manner.

Mughal style even extended its sway further to the south. Towards the end of the 18th century the Muslim usurpers of the Karnataka kingdom of Mysore, Haidar Ali and Tipu Sultan, also took pains to create a Mughal-inspired environment, to the extent of adopting Persian as the official court language. Tipu's garden palace at Srirangapatnam outside Mysore was inspired by Mughal architecture; so too his personal weapons and jewels. Thus did Mughal style survive the decline of the Mughal empire so as to pervade almost the whole of India.

FOLLOWING PAGES The finest of all Mughal-styled *shish mahals*, or mirrored halls, is Jai Mandir at Amber built by Mirza Raja Jai Singh, a Rajput ruler who enjoyed a successful career under Shah Jahan and Aurangzeb. Like other rulers of Rajasthan who were employed by the Mughals, Mirza Raja Jai Singh was responsible for introducing Mughal style to Rajasthan.

MATERIALS & TECHNIQUES

An extraordinarily impressive diversity of materials and techniques went into the creation of Mughal style – in architecture, painting, textiles and all the other arts that produced objects of beauty. The virtuosity with which the different themes of Mughal style take visual form, whether in polychrome stonework, ink and watercolour washes, woven silks, gold and silver inlays, or carved jade and ivory, remains unmatched in the entire history of Indian architecture and art. Such an achievement is a tribute to the direct personal involvement of the Mughal emperors, their family members and nobles in the supervision of monumental building projects and in the everyday functioning of the imperial *karkhanas*, where highly skilled calligraphers, painters, weavers, embroiderers, metalworkers, jewellers, goldsmiths and ivory carvers were employed by the thousand. The results of this patronage are evident in the aesthetic and technical achievements of the buildings that still stand, and the many exquisitely crafted, luxurious objects that miraculously survived the decline and ultimate disintegration of the Mughal court.

SANDSTONE & MARBLE

Nowhere is the fusion of Central Asian and Persian models with indigenous materials and techniques better demonstrated than in the stonework that covers so many august Mughal monuments. By far the most popular cladding is the deep mottled red sandstone found in the area around Agra. This makes an early appearance under Akbar, and thereafter becomes the preferred imperial building material. Employed for the ramparts of royal citadels, it even lends its name to the various Lal Qilas, or Red Forts, erected by Akbar and his successors in Agra, Delhi and Lahore. But already in Humayun's tomb in Delhi this red sandstone is modified by white marble and yellow sandstone to highlight the arched profiles of the main portals. This predilection for different hued masonry initiates a tendency towards multi-coloured effects that reaches a climax during Jahangir's reign. The gateway that this emperor erected for his father's mausoleum at Sikandra presents bold geometric and floral patterns, realized in different coloured stones.

In Itimad-ad Daula's tomb on the riverfront at Agra the colour scheme is dominated by white marble, into which are set diverse stones, including specimens with varied skeins of colour and texture, brought from distant quarries in Central India expressly for this purpose. These materials create geometric patterns of different designs, as well as arabesque motifs contained in multi-lobed cartouches. The overall effect of complexity is modified by the white marble backing that ensures an overall pale delicacy. Transported to Agra from Makrana in Rajasthan, more than 350 kilometres away, this same white marble is used in

Vivid designs composed of assorted marbles and sandstones entirely cover the facade of the entrance gateway to Akbar's tomb at Sikandra. The contrasting colours of the different stones help visually distinguish the individual design components, transforming the building into a veritable catalogue of boldly conceived, polychrome geometric patterns.

the Taj Mahal. The dazzlingly pure effect of this domed tomb and its complementary quartet of ornamental minarets is accentuated by the red sandstone that cloaks the mosque and matching structure that stand at either side of the tomb, as well as the entrance gateway and pavilions of the great *char-bagh* garden in front. The marble screens encasing the cenotaphs inside the mausoleum, and even the cenotaphs themselves, are decorated with *pietra dura* work of the finest quality. Here lapis lazuli, jade, carnelian, jasper and various agates are cut into tiny pieces and assembled into the forms of naturalistic flowers and arabesque traceries of unsurpassed delicacy. Equally sophisticated *pietra dura* work was employed by Shah Jahan in the marble pavilions that he erected in his fortified palaces at Agra and Delhi.

While such colouristic stone effects may be regarded as the technical high point of Mughal style in its architectural expression, monochrome textures were also exploited for visual effect. Boldly chiselled geometric patterns and arabesque flourishes animate the red sandstone columns and facades of Akbar's palaces at Agra and Fatehpur Sikri. In Shah Jahan's buildings white marble was delicately sculpted to achieve shallow relief representations of flowering plants, sometimes bunched together in ornate vases. The remarkably lifelike renditions of such motifs are proof of the age-old abilities of Indian stonemasons to accurately reproduce natural forms. Perforated *jali* screens offer further evidence of the exceptional capabilities of local masons. They are carved with the utmost virtuosity into geometric designs or stylized floral motifs that continue uninterruptedly, and virtually imperceptibly, across the different slabs of sandstone or marble. Filtering the harsh glare of the noonday sun or the soft rays of moonlight, the *jalis* throw intriguing shadows to create ever-changing patterns. The Mughals' masterly treatment of the *jali* reveals the traditional Islamic preoccupation with light and light symbolism. No wonder that such screens are ideally suited to encase the corridors that run around the tomb chambers of revered emperors and holy saints.

PLASTERWORK, TILES & MIRRORS

Where stone was deemed too costly or where masonry building traditions were never firmly established, as in the provinces of Punjab and Sindh, plaster and tilework were preferred. Plaster was embellished with finely-cut relief detail, often in fluid arabesque designs set into the lozenge-shaped stalactite facets that fill the half-domed interiors of arched portals, or which cover the ceilings of domed chambers in mosques and tombs. Outlines of long-necked drinking vessels are popular, generally etched as deep niches into plasterwork, as if to accommodate actual bottles of glass or brass, or sometimes merely suggested in shallow relief. Plaster also served as a base for the mural paintings that adorn the interiors of palaces and tomb chambers. Floral motifs predominate here, either as sprays of flowers in vases, or as repeated blossoms set within ornamental lattices and linked by trailing stalks. Blues, greens and yellows are preferred, highlighted with gold, with occasional vermillion and turquoise flourishes to achieve the vivid colouristic palette that is a hallmark of Mughal style. More intensely coloured and generally better preserved are the ceramic tiles that adorn Mughal religious and civic monuments, such as those in Lahore, where polychrome tilework had a long history extending back to pre-Mughal times. The finest Mughal tiles are composite mosaics of differently coloured, cut-out pieces, each fired to the optimum temperature to produce the most brilliant results. Tile compositions of this type have floral designs, geometric interlacings and even calligraphic passages on bright yellow, turquoise or white backgrounds. Even animal motifs are found, as on the outer walls of the Mughal fort in Lahore. Other tiles are fired according to the *cuerda seca* method. Here, different colours are applied to the same square area, but separated by greased lines that dissolve when the tile is fired. This technique is well suited to floral compositions spreading over large groups of tiles.

Even more spectacular are the effects achieved by the use of mirrors set into plaster to produce glittering facades, such as those with floral panels set within arched niches. Mirrored pieces also enhance the interiors of Mughal palaces, notably the delightful *shish mahals*. In order to produce the maximum number of reflecting surfaces, minute pieces of mirror are glued to the interlocking facets of the vaults and domes with which these halls are roofed. As already noted the most impressive example of all Mughal styled *shish mahals* is that built by the Rajput ruler Mirza Raja Jai Singh in his palace at Amber in Rajasthan.

PAINTING ON PAPER

The production of paintings on paper to illustrate Persian and Indian literary classics, as well as works of philosophy, science and history, was initiated under Akbar. Many artists were recruited into the imperial *kitabkhanas* so as to generate large numbers of miniature illustrations for Persian epics and Indian fables, as well as for historical chronicles like the *Akbar Nama*, recording events of Akbar's own reign, imitated later by Shah Jahan in his *Padshah Nama*. This enterprise was only possible thanks to the professional organization of workshops under the guidance of a team of studio masters who discussed with the emperors which legends and biographical narratives were to be illustrated, and the specific scenes to be depicted. Different artists were responsible for sketching the overall compositions in black or ochre linework, filling in the details of figures and faces by applying opaque watercolour paint, and adding the background or border details, generally in more transparent and paler tones. Assistants prepared the different pigments by grinding and mixing appropriate mineral and vegetable sources; they also burnished the different layers of paint by rubbing the pages with polished stone to achieve the required gloss. Gold highlights were added as required. At first this work came under the direction of the Persian masters who were brought to India by Humayun, but eventually native talent prevailed.

While the exquisitely painted historical scenes and contemporary portraits that issued forth from the *kitabkhanas* of Akbar, Jahangir and Shah Jahan may be considered the climax of Mughal pictorial art, it is the decorative aspects of miniatures that relate most closely to the other arts that constitute Mughal style. Calligraphy is accorded the highest importance, with an emphasis on *qit'as*, or display pages. Here, Koranic passages and poetic verses, generally executed in the fluid *nasta`liq* script much beloved by the most proficient calligraphers, are surrounded by a delicate floral decor, sometimes sprinkled liberally with gold. Contrasting scripts are combined on a single page so as to showcase the virtuoso capabilities of an individual artist, who usually signed himself in one corner. Different specialists were responsible for the intricate arabesque linework that embellishes the borders of calligraphic pages. The sinuous motifs are executed in delicate brushwork and filled with luminous gold, blue and pink tones. Arabesque designs are sometimes expanded into major compositions in their own right, perhaps framing the opening lines of a Koranic chapter, or the titles of an imperial patron.

Calligraphic compositions and arabesque motifs in Mughal painting inevitably remain close to Persian pictorial precedent. In contrast, the flowers, animals and birds that appear in miniatures are animated by a naturalism that is quintessentially Indian, especially the flora and fauna that are depicted in the borders surrounding the central compositions. Flowers of different types are aligned in rows, as if to suggest the plots of an imaginary garden. Their petals and leaves are depicted in a lifelike manner, employing the multitudinous hues drawn from nature. Alternatively they are represented in delicate monochrome, perhaps in gold on a dark blue or green background, so as not to compete visually with the central narrative scene or calligraphic quotation. Blossoms and interlacing curling leafy stems are combined to form elegant designs that are perfectly suited to borders. Flowers even become the principal subject of pictorial compositions, especially those commissioned by Jahangir that were inspired by European botanical studies. Here tulips, irises, poppies and other species are portrayed with the greatest faithfulness, usually against a blank background so as to capture all of their details with maximum clarity.

Paintings of animals and birds dating from Jahangir's era are depicted with a comparable realism that truly earns them the status of portraits. They include studies of *nilgai*, lions, cows, goats, zebras and even squirrels; birds are represented by falcons, peacocks, pheasants and herons. A no less varied menagerie populates the delicately executed borders of miniatures, sometimes in the company of *simurghs*, the fantastic flying creatures of Chinese origin that were conveyed to India via Persian art. Humans occasionally intrude into these animal compositions, especially as hunters with dogs pursuing deer. Such scenes sometimes become major compositions in their own right, especially when painted in brightly toned lacquer on the lids of wooden cabinets.

CARPETS & TEXTILES

Though now completely stripped of their magnificent textiles, the palaces of the Mughals were once clad in vividly patterned carpets, cushions, hangings and awnings fashioned out of wool, silk and cotton. The mobile camps in which the emperors spent considerable time planning their military campaigns, receiving visitors and hosting entertainments were elaborate textile structures that replicated the layouts and decorative schemes of their more permanent masonry residences in Agra, Delhi or Lahore. The costumes that rulers and courtiers wore on formal occasions were equally splendid. Though only a fraction of these carpets, textiles and costumes survive intact, they are accurately depicted in the miniatures of the period. These pictorial records confirm that these gorgeous cloths played a central role in creating the splendid environments in which the Mughal emperors conducted the formal business of their everyday lives, let alone their more private pursuits and pleasures.

Densely knotted carpets fashioned in the finest Safavid manner, with woollen piles and cotton or silk warps and wefts, were first woven at the *karkhanas* set up for Akbar by Persian masters, and later by locally trained specialists. Intended for royal audience halls and private apartments, as well as for the grandest mosques and shrines of the era, Mughal carpets had complex designs and took months to complete. Surviving examples have floral or arabesque borders that surround a central field filled with flowering plants aligned in rows, or contained in compartments defined by lattice frames. The backgrounds of the central panels are invariably in vivid red, recalling the red sandstone reserved for official Mughal buildings. More unusual are the carpets with landscape scenes inhabited by naturalistic animals and birds, even the occasional fantastic creature, surrounded by lifelike palm trees and flowering bushes, also on red backgrounds. Scenes with animals locked in savage combat or with hunters pursuing fleeing deer make an occasional appearance in the woven compositions of the period, though these motifs are generally accorded minor importance.

In summers, the floors of the Mughal palaces were covered with lighter cotton spreads produced by the time-consuming combination of dyeing, printing and free-hand painting techniques known as *kalamkari*. Apart from being used as coverings and hangings in Mughal palaces, these cloths also constituted a significant component of the lucrative textile trade conducted by agents of the Mughal emperors to South-east Asia and later to Europe. These lightweight cloths were invariably decorated with floral motifs, including the ubiquitous flowers-in-vase motif.

Among the most lavish and expensive textiles that issued from workshops at provincial textile centres such as Ahmedabad, Cambay, Banaras and Dacca were velvets, brocades, silks and satins. These cloths were required not only to furnish the audience halls and private apartments with canopies, curtains, wall hangings and cushions, but also for the rich apparel of the emperor and his nobles – their elaborate *sherwanis* and *jamas*. As with *kalamkaris*, floral designs were preferred, most often consisting of regularly spaced, single flowers, woven or block printed onto a plain background. The hot summers made demands for the sheerest cottons, which the Mughals also ordered. After the conquest of Bengal in 1575, the Mughals discovered the region's famous *malmal*, or muslin, and the complex white-on-white *jamdani* weaving and *chikan* embroidery. And, since they delighted in delicacy, they spurred the production of these superbly subtle fabrics.

The Mughal emperors adhered to the Islamic tradition of *khilat*, or robes of honour, to reward superior service or to gift to special guests. For this purpose they often commissioned the famous Kashmiri *jamewar* shawls, and it is to the development of these masterpieces of the weavers' art that the Mughals made their greatest contribution in the textile sphere. Under Akbar the Kashmiri shawl, with its borders of brilliantly coloured floral motifs, acquired particular popularity, the practice of wearing these shawls becoming obligatory. Abu'l Fazl describes in considerable detail how Akbar transformed the shawl industry by ensuring that particular styles were adopted at his court.

METALWORK, ARMS & JEWELRY

No account of Mughal style would be complete without acknowledging the outstanding accomplishments of Indian metalworkers. Skilled craftsmen throughout the empire produced meticulously crafted vessels out of gold, silver and brass that were used personally by the emperors and their nobles and commanders, and were also given as gifts on ceremonial occasions. The sheer variety of these vessels is impressive: ewers with spherical bodies enhanced by flutings or swirling facets, and long spouts ending in animal heads; water basins and spittoons with bulbous bases and projecting flanges; long-necked wine flasks with spherical bodies, sometimes divided into facets; circular beakers with dome-like covers imitating European vessels; bulbous *huqqa* bases seated on metallic rings; circular trays with geometric floral patterns arranged in radial fashion; octagonal boxes with curving lids for storing *pan* that was enjoyed after a meal. These metallic artefacts are usually adorned with arabesque and floral motifs, either engraved directly into the metal to achieve complex linear designs, or hammered in relief to achieve embossed surfaces. Such designs are also inlaid with silver and brass in a laborious technique known as *bidri*, after the town of Bidar in the Deccan where this method originated, but which probably flourished at other centres throughout the region. *Bidri* wares are unsurpassed for their spectacular lustrous surfaces, with gleaming highlights of zigzags, petals or blossoms on dark metallic backgrounds composed mainly of zinc, with some copper and lead. These patterns are imitated in gold paint on the dark green and blue glass *huqqa* bowls that were also produced at the Mughal *karkhanas*. They were even sometimes realized in embossed brass sheets that covered wooden furniture and doors.

Though inspired by European models, this silver beaker with a curved lid was produced at an Indian workshop at some date in the second half of the 17th century. The beaker is engraved and chased with floral motifs that were probably intended to receive brightly coloured enamelled inlays. Such motifs are similar to those found in stone relief carving and the painted borders of manuscripts. CATALOGUE 78

Another metallic art that makes an appearance in Mughal style is that of enamelling. Supposedly of European origin, enamelling was taken up at *karkhanas* at Agra, Delhi and Lahore, as well as at other workshops of the empire, especially those in Lucknow during the 18th century. According to this technique, shining pieces of glass were fused at high temperatures onto a metal base. Dishes, basins, trays and *huqqa* bowls decorated according to this method all employ brilliant red, blue, green and yellow enamel inlays to create designs with interweaving petals and leaves. These motifs contrast with the gold, silver and copper surfaces onto which they are applied; in some cases these enamelled floral motifs cover the entire body of a basin or *huqqa* bowl. While blossoms and leaves are the most commonplace enamelled designs, some bowls and spice boxes are animated by birds and animals set in imaginary landscapes, all executed in luminous colours.

Arms and armour, though obviously intended for the demands of warfare, are also the vehicle for displays of virtuoso metalwork. Magnificently ornamented daggers, swords and shields were worn by nobles at formal audiences in the presence of the emperor and were also much sought after as prestigious gifts. Steel blades of the hardest quality, sometimes of European origin, have stamped or inlaid inscriptions giving the name and titles of the owner. These inscriptions are often hammered in gold or brass directly into the blade according to the technique known as damascening, imported into India from the Middle East. Hilts and handles are overlaid or inlaid with silver and gold designs, often of blossoms and leaves that present a striking contrast to the dark iron or steel base metal. Polychrome enamels also make an appearance in the arms of the era, best seen in the gleaming leafy designs that adorn metallic hilts and scabbards of swords and daggers.

Foreign travellers to India during the Mughal era were all dazzled by the brilliance of Indian jewelry, leading one observer to describe the country as 'an abyss of gold'. The splendour of Mughal jewelry, as worn by the emperor himself and his nobles on ceremonial occasions, is recorded in the miniature paintings of the period; regrettably, there is little pictorial record of the jewels worn by the queens and most important female members of the imperial household, though these can hardly have been less spectacular. In addition to shaping and engraving individual gems of great worth, especially imported emeralds and rubies, the chief task of Mughal jewellers was to assemble different gems into dense compositions according to the *kundan* technique. Here diamonds, emeralds and rubies are set into gold frames, the gems being separated by tiny gold strips, to create dense assortments of precious stones. These are often arranged as floral sprays, sometimes also as leaf-like formations with curving pointed tips. Necklaces with multiple pendants, earrings, bracelets and finger-rings are all fashioned according to this method; so too the flamboyant feather-like *kalgi*, or plume-like ornament with pendant pearls or rubies, that adorned royal turbans and the no less ornate *sarpech*.

JADE, IVORY & MOTHER-OF-PEARL

The Mughal emperors were inveterate collectors of jade objects. However, since almost no jade was available in India this material had to be imported at considerable expense from Central Asia and China. Milky white nephrite jade and opaque, deep green jade, as well as other hard stones such as agate and crystal, were expertly carved by Mughal craftsmen into a variety of elegantly shaped, luxurious objects. They include bowls and wine cups carved with leafy swirls or symmetrical lobes that suggest full lotus blooms, or engraved in delicate relief with the outlines of blossoms and petals. That such drinking vessels were fashioned for the emperors themselves is confirmed by the imperial names and titles that are sometimes inscribed on their sides and rims. Writing boxes and ink stands intended for imperial use are also fashioned out of jade; so too mirror-backs and *huqqa* bases. Many of these objects are inlaid with rubies, emeralds and pieces of lapis lazuli set in the semblance of floral sprays, or as trellis patterns outlined by thin gold strips. Miniature blossoms of rubies and diamonds are inset into the jade hilts of daggers and knives to create weapons with spectacular decorations. Such gems even highlight the eyes and other features of the miniature lifelike heads of animals that adorn some jade hilts.

Ivory is another material that was much appreciated by Mughal craftsmen. Primer flasks used for storing gunpowder when on hunting expeditions maintain the curved profiles of the elephant tusks out of which they are fashioned. Their sides, however, are covered with relief compositions that mingle different animals, such as lions, deer and antelopes with different types of birds; there are even minute scenes of animal fights and of human hunters carrying their spoils. Pieces of ivory also serve as decorative inlays set into wooden chests and writing cabinets, a technique perfected by craftsmen in Sindh. Repeated flowers in ivory inlays replicate similar designs on woven garden carpets and the borders of *patkas,* or printed waist-sashes, worn by the emperor and his nobles.

Because of its lustrous qualities, mother-of-pearl makes a special contribution to Mughal style. In Mughal times the graves of the much venerated Chishti saints in Ahmedabad, Fatehpur Sikri and Delhi were provided with wooden canopies cloaked in densely patterned, mother-of-pearl inlays. Like the similarly decorated wooden furniture, much of it manufactured for the Ottoman Turkish market, these canopies were manufactured in Gujarat. Caskets with angled tops as well as writing chests and pen boxes are adorned with mother-of-pearl designs of swirling arabesques, or of split-leaves and rosettes; one example is even covered with lines of calligraphy quoting verses of Persian poetry. The shimmering surfaces of these canopies and items of furniture rival the splendour of the finest architectural ornamentation and decorative arts of the era. They offer yet another instance of the outstanding technical and aesthetic accomplishments of the masons, artists and craftsmen who were responsible for the creation of Mughal style.

FOLLOWING PAGES Gleaming mother-of-pearl inlays enhance the top of this casket, made in Gujarat in 1587. The elegant arabesque swirls with regularly disposed five-petalled blossoms not only fill the central lobed cartouche, but extend all the way to the edge of the rectangular lid in a continuous design. The lustrous pink and turquoise shell pieces contrast dramatically with the dark wooden body of the lid. CATALOGUE 15

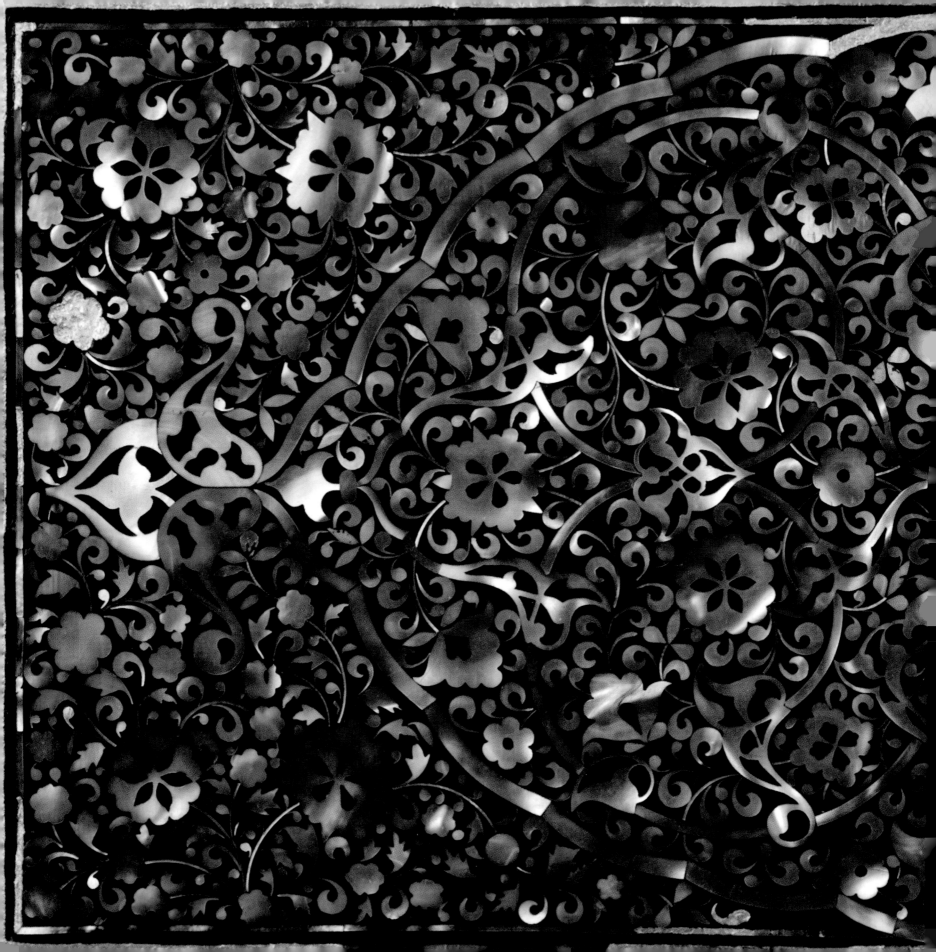

Colour Portfolio

IMPERIAL RED (pp. 50—51)

The mottled, deep red sandstone mined in the quarries outside Agra was the first building material to be used widely by Mughal architects. It cloaked the ramparts of the great fortresses of Agra and Delhi, and was even used for this wall panel portraying an imaginary landscape in the Turkish Sultana's house in Akbar's palace city at Fatehpur Sikri. Brilliant red was also the colour of the imperial tents in which the Mughal emperors lived for many months each year, either on military campaigns or on tours of their domains. Such a colouristic signal of the Mughal presence came to be identified with the emperor himself and his official place of residence.

WHITE ON WHITE (pp. 52—53)

White marble assumes a quite different role to that of red sandstone in Mughal style, since it symbolizes purity, goodness and spirituality, according to the orthodox Islamic tradition. Akbar used white marble for the dome of his father's tomb in Delhi as well as for the mausoleum of Shaykh Salim Chishti at Fatehpur Sikri, while Shah Jahan chose it for the Taj Mahal, the supremely ambitious project of his reign, from where come these flower panels. While colouristic effects are used throughout the decoration of the Taj Mahal, it is these unblemished white on white relief carvings that best express Shah Jahan's devotion for his beloved wife Mumtaz Mahal.

BLACK & OCHRE ON WHITE (pp. 54—55)

The cutting and assemblage of stones of different colours to create rich polychrome designs remains one of the outstanding technical and aesthetic achievements of Mughal style. Among the diverse polychrome patterns that adorn the tomb of Itimad-ad Daula in Agra are complex geometric shapes composed of interlocking stars and multi-pronged elements. Cut out of black masonry and ochre coloured fossilized stones from Central India, many with variegated veins and roughly textured surfaces, these shapes are laid into a white marble background, thereby creating the desired black and ochre on white scheme that characterizes the exterior of the monument.

ORANGE & WHITE ON YELLOW & GREEN (pp. 56—57)

The monuments in Punjab are adorned with shimmering polychrome glazed tiles, a technique that thrived in this province of the Mughal empire, and which was closely related to Central Asian and Persian practice. These two square tiles from a mid–17th–century tomb in Lahore have flowers with orange and white blossoms and green leaves floating on bright yellow and green backgrounds. The colours are applied in the *cuerda seca* technique, the coloured glazes being differentiated by greased strips that dissolve when the tiles are fired. The thin dark lines left after the firing delineate the petals and leaves, imbuing the flowers with a lyrical naturalism. CATALOGUE 41 & 42

RED ON GOLD (pp. 58—59)

Red was often utilized for smaller objects fashioned for the emperor's personal use, such as this 17th-century gold tray enhanced by brilliant red enamel inlays, possibly intended for a small circular box for *pan*. Though darker coloured enamels are used for the leafy stalks of the flowers it is the red blossoms on a gleaming gold background that prevail, giving the circular tray its overall spectacular tonal quality. The prevailing red touches of the spreading floral design indicate that this object almost certainly belonged to the imperial treasury. Only a few such items from the Mughal era have survived into modern times. CATALOGUE 89

GREEN & BLUE ON WHITE (pp. 60—61)

One of the most lavish combinations of materials to be found anywhere in Mughal style is that which juxtaposes semiprecious stones with jade. Here a diagonal lattice consisting of single leaves crafted out of pieces of deep green jade and defined by minute gold strips entirely covers the curving body of a white jade *huqqa* bowl. The lattice serves as a frame for single flowers with pointed petals created out of lapis lazuli, also contained in gold strips. Both the leaves and flowers are moulded in shallow relief, in contrast to the smoothly polished, milky white body of the bowl itself. It is, however, the colouristic accents of deep green and bright blue that prevail. CATALOGUE 65

GREEN ON GOLD & GOLD ON GREEN (pp. 62—63)

Huqqa bowls for pipes to smoke tobacco became fashionable in India after tobacco was introduced to the Mughal court by the Portuguese. Green glass *huqqa* bowls dating from the late 17th and early 18th century were painted with gold, and then etched so as to reveal green leafy motifs on a gold background, or gilt poppy flowers on a green background. In both combinations, the applied gold paint is highlighted by the contrasting dark green background of the glass. Such colour schemes were an essential component of the objects used by the emperor and his nobles, a perfect accompaniment to the smoking of tobacco and other pleasures. CATALOGUE 43 & 44

YELLOW & BLUE ON RED (pp. 64—65)

As has already been pointed out, red was the colour reserved for the Mughal emperor and his court. For this reason it dominated the designs of the textiles that were displayed in the imperial audience halls and pleasure pavilions, none more impressive that the magnificently woven carpets on which the ruler would place his throne. This early 17th-century carpet has a repeating pattern of scrolling vines and blossoms arranged in mirror symmetry across the central panel. Related tones of yellow and blue are supplemented by the white and grey flourishes of the leaves and petals. These colours are dominated throughout by the brilliance of the red background. CATALOGUE 24

THEMES

EOMETRY

Mughal style is continually underpinned by a strict geometric structure in accordance
with the arts of the wider Islamic world, including those of Central Asia and Persia which
had the most direct impact on India. A sense of mathematics is always present, even in
more seemingly fluid compositions of arabesques, or naturalistic assemblages of flowers
and plants. The faith in geometry as a governing principle of design is shared equally by
Mughal builders and the artists employed in the imperial *karkhanas*, though it is perhaps
most obvious in architecture. The mathematical basis of the mosques, tombs and pleasure
pavilions erected by Mughal emperors is expressed in the rigorous symmetry of their plans
and the majestic proportions of their elevations, all invariably dictated by the manipulation
of regulating units of measurement.

From the Islamic tradition the Mughals also inherited beliefs about the meanings of
certain geometric figures: the circle is supposed to represent the dome of heaven; the
octagon the *hasht bihisht*, or Eight Paradises; the chevron the flowing waters of the streams
of paradise that traverse the *char-bagh*, or four-square paradisiacal garden. Geometry was
never a mere adornment of Mughal style; rather, it was a means of evoking a world that
lay beyond earthly experience. Since the universe itself was believed to have an underlying
numerical structure, the fact that architecture and the arts are both mathematically based
was a device for imbuing the works of man with a transcendent quality — a veritable
paradise on earth. Furthermore, the fact that geometric patterns are capable of endless
extension was a constant reminder of the infinity of the universe. It is hardly surpising,
then, that such designs are ubiquitous in Mughal style. In Mughal architecture geometric
patterns expressed the essential mathematical basis of a building plan; but they could
also be extended horizontally to cover the pavements and walkways that led away from
the structure itself into the surrounding garden terraces, thereby linking architecture

with nature. This was an essential requirement both in the great garden tombs of the emperors and their queens, and in the royal apartments that opened onto private *char-baghs*. Geometric patterns were also capable of being extended vertically to fill architectural panels and *jali* screens – thereby imparting visual interest and variety to the building elevation; with ingenious manipulation such patterns could even cover the curving surfaces of internal vaults and domes. On a miniature scale, the same designs decorated the circular interiors of dishes or the swelling surfaces of jars and bowls.

Geometric design in Mughal style may at first appear to present an inexhaustible range of patterns. However, these are based on different permutations of a limited series of comparatively simple components; notably, polygons and stars with five, six, eight, ten or twelve sides or points. The seemingly never-ending range of patterns in the architecture and fine arts of the period can, in fact, be reduced to inventive manipulations of these polygons and stars. In order to create continuous geometric 'fields' some of the intermediate shapes must need necessarily be irregular; however, they are employed again and again so as to create designs that achieve visual coherence. The sheer variety of geometric patterns in Mughal style means that there is never any question of deadening repetition; to the contrary, masons and craftsmen are inclined to flaunt their command of mathematics by presenting a miscellany of geometric patterns, as if to explore all the different combinations that are possible using the same components. The aesthetic effect is invariably that of harmony, since the geometric patterns are composed of repeated figures that create an underlying visual consistency; the sheer range of patterns guarantees constant visual stimulation.

While the principles of geometric design in Mughal style are commonly found throughout the Islamic world, the patterns used in India may be distinguished from those that appear

Patterns with geometrically determined, blue and white zigzags are woven into the overall pattern of this 18th-century shawl. In architecture, similar chevron designs created in relief stonework or out of different coloured stone inlays symbolize flowing water. Here the chevron design was used to embellish a large woollen shawl. CATALOGUE 28

in the buildings and arts of other Muslim countries through their expression in indigenous materials, textures and colours. Polygons and multi-pointed stars in Mughal style may appear in identical or similar geometric configurations to those found in the arts of Central Asia and Persia, but in the hands of Mughal masons and artisans this geometry attains an unmistakable Indian personality. This is most obvious in the use of white marble set into red sandstone to achieve polychrome patterns of startlingly colouristic and textural boldness. Here the shapes of the various polygons and stars are accentuated by the contrast between the comparatively rough surface of the red sandstone and the shining smooth surface of the white marble. In order to achieve yet further variety, architects introduced colour effects through the use of yellow sandstone and black stone to accomplish dense polychrome effects. The result sometimes recalls a richly toned textile more than a laborious work of inlaid masonry. Nowhere is this better seen than in the inlaid stonework of the wall panels of the gateway to Akbar's tomb at Sikandra and the tomb of Itimad-ad Daula in Agra. Coloured tilework applied to brick masonry is also used in geometric design, as in the monuments in and around Lahore, where this technique was common. Occasionally in such designs, some bricks are left unglazed, but deeply cut with geometric patterns so as to achieve striking contrasts of colour and texture. Elsewhere, sandstone wall panels are carved to create patterns in different planes, the different geometric modules in relief being distinguished by brightly toned paintwork.

Geometric designs are also ideally suited to the perforated *jali* screens that admit light to the corridors surrounding the tombs of Mughal emperors and saints. While such screens were common in the Muslim architecture of pre-Mughal India, especially that which flourished in Gujarat, in the hands of Mughal craftsmen *jalis* become showpieces of virtuoso stone-cutting with intricate geometric designs. The screens in Itimad-ad Daula's tomb, for instance, present dense arrays of interlocking hexagons, of six-pointed stars alternating with hexagons, and of twelve-pointed stars. The interiors of these figures are generally filled with delicate honeycomb patterns that visually 'soften' the regulating geometry, so as to realize a consistent, perforated texture that filters the harsh Indian sun. Most of these figures are based on the manipulation of equilateral triangles, with repeated angles of 30 or 60 degrees. This establishes a unifying grid that lends visual coherence to the various patterns.

Because they occupy curving spaces, the vaults and domes of Mughal architecture are sometimes the settings of highly complicated geometries. A particular case is the use of stalactite-like facets set at angles to each other in different planes to achieve complex three-dimensional designs. Mughal architects employed such stalactites to achieve a visually seamless transition from the vertical surfaces of the walls beneath to the apexes of the curving arches or domes above. Such stalactite compositions were generally modelled on Central Asian and Persian building practice, where they were known as *qalib kari*, or 'mouldwork'. In the hands of Indian craftsmen, however, stalactite vaults become vehicles for a vivid floral decor, composed of coloured tile panels or painted plasterwork, tightly contained in interlocking geometric shapes. Though such three-dimensional patterns may appear at first to defy analysis, they are in actuality composed of dense and ingenious manipulations of repeated components, most often lozenge-shaped elements with long sides and indented short sides. When it comes to domes, Mughal architects often selected radial designs with interlocking arcs, spiralling outwards from a central swirling medallion. The radial arms in such compositions sometimes take on a vegetal quality, being treated as interlaced stalks with leafy protuberances. Whether the arcs are plain or treated in a vegetal manner, the overall effect of such patterns is that of continuous expansion. The same is true of radial designs at a diminutive scale, as in trays and dishes with gleaming metallic inlays, with the central fields filled with concentric rings of petals or chevrons. Such designs inevitably enhance the circular frames in which they are set.

Geometrically based frames and lattices containing floral ornament, whether complete plants or merely petals or blossoms, constitute another important dimension of Mughal style, both in architectural decoration and the fine arts. Such regulating structures are generally based on repeated circles or diamond-shaped compartments defined by interlocking double-curved and looped bands. These bands are often treated as stalks with leafy extensions, with flowers marking the intersections of the different elements. Sometimes the bands are replaced by stalk-like ribbons in regular diamond-like formation. However, such plant-like transformations never obscure the underlying purpose of the lattices and frames, which is to divide areas of different shapes into repeated, mathematically regulated components. This is true of the lattices and frames that cover extensive flat surfaces, such as carpets or ceilings, or which wrap around the swelling bodies of jars and bowls. In one semicircular panel in the Khass Mahal in the private apartment of Shah Jahan's imperial residence in Delhi, for example, looped lattices frame the relief representation of the scales of justice that serves as an insignia of the imperial figure himself.

The fact that lattices and frames in Mughal style so often become the vehicle of vegetal ornament may partly be attributed to European influence, especially of Italianate art, where such designs were common in the 16th and 17th centuries. These motifs were probably transmitted to India via the illustrated books and precious objects presented as gifts by European envoys to the Mughal court. In the hands of Mughal artisans, however, such Westernized geometries become Indianized by the application of an irrepressible floral decor. Nowhere is this better demonstrated than in the carpets, *jalis* and ceilings with continuous foliated lattices mostly laid out on a diagonal grid (*see* endpapers). As elsewhere these elements are regulated by a mathematical structure that confirms yet again the geometric basis of Mughal style.

Geometric patterns in alternating red sandstone and white marble pieces present bold colouristic contrasts ideally suited to architectural settings. The plinth on which the Taj Mahal is raised above the bank of the Yamuna River at Agra employs repeated white octagons filled with red four-pointed stars, here shown somewhat distorted in perspective (**left**); while red six-pointed stars surrounded by groups of white hexagons are utilized at Akbar's tomb at Sikandra (**right**). Whether based on six- or eight-sided figures, such mathematical patterns are infinitely expandable, and therefore appropriate for terraces and walkways.

Wall panels on the imposing gate of Akbar's tomb present a veritable kaleidoscope of geometries, created in red sandstone and white marble, with yellow sandstone and black stone additions. This variety of materials achieves rich polychrome effects that emphasize the different design elements. One pattern has ten-pointed stars surrounded by interlocking rings of pentagons (**left**); others have central stars with eight, ten or twelve points defined by lines that are extended to the edges of the frames, thereby creating complex geometrical grids (**centre & opposite**).

Equally diverse are the geometric designs created in different coloured stones set into white marble on the tomb of Itimad-ad Daula. Many of these polychrome patterns are generated from repeated six-pointed stars, alternating with hexagons, separated by two-pronged angled elements. The panels are surrounded by bands of interweaving arabesque scrolls, the strands being distinguished by different coloured stonework. Such two-dimensional geometries alternate with monochrome *jali* screens that present additional, but no less complex mathematical patterns (*see* pp. 82—85).

Among the other geometries that enliven Itimad-ad Daula's tomb are panels with twelve-pointed stars in white marble containing six-lobed flowers. The stars are surrounded by rings of pointed, lozenge-shaped elements, which in turn generate trios of smaller lozenge-shaped components, the last distinguished by richly veined, dark fossilized stone (**opposite**). On the Taj Mahal, eight-pointed stars created from rotated squares are framed by black and yellow bands; these create zigzag designs that serve as framing borders (**left**).

FOLLOWING PAGES Patterns based on the pentagon also play a role in the geometric decor of Itimad-ad Daula's tomb. Rings of lozenge-shaped black elements, creating ten-pointed stars with yellow floral points in the middle, are surrounded by smaller, five-pointed stars in yellow. Since the ten-pointed stars are disposed on a diagonal grid, the rings of yellow five-pointed stars interlock in a complex sharing of circular fields. An overall effect of visual lightness is guaranteed by the white marble background.

In addition to the two-dimensional, polychrome geometries of its wall panels, Itimad-ad Daula's tomb also employs perforated *jali* screens worked with the utmost virtuosity. Chiselled out of interlocking white marble slabs, the joints of which are virtually invisible, the screens create a delicate mesh that filters the light entering the tomb chamber. The designs include ten-pointed stars, within ten-sided figures set on a diagonal grid (**opposite**), as well as interlocking hexagons filled with a honeycomb pattern (**below right**) and six-pointed stars alternating with hexagons (**below left**).

FOLLOWING PAGES Another geometric configuration that occurs in the *jalis* of Itimad-ad Daula's tomb is a grid of zigzag bands based on a 'deconstructed' octagon. Here, four out of eight of the outward-pointing sides of an octagon, set at a diagonal to the frame, are combined with four inward pointed sides so as to create eight-sided figures that interlock both horizontally and vertically in an ever-expanding pattern. The interiors of these figures have a honeycomb filigree that contributes a more delicate, secondary geometric dimension that complements the principal zigzag bands.

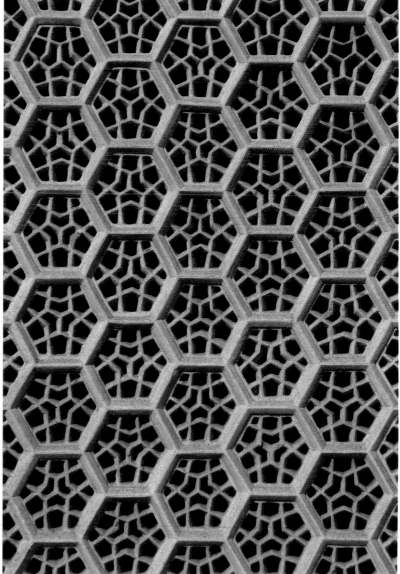

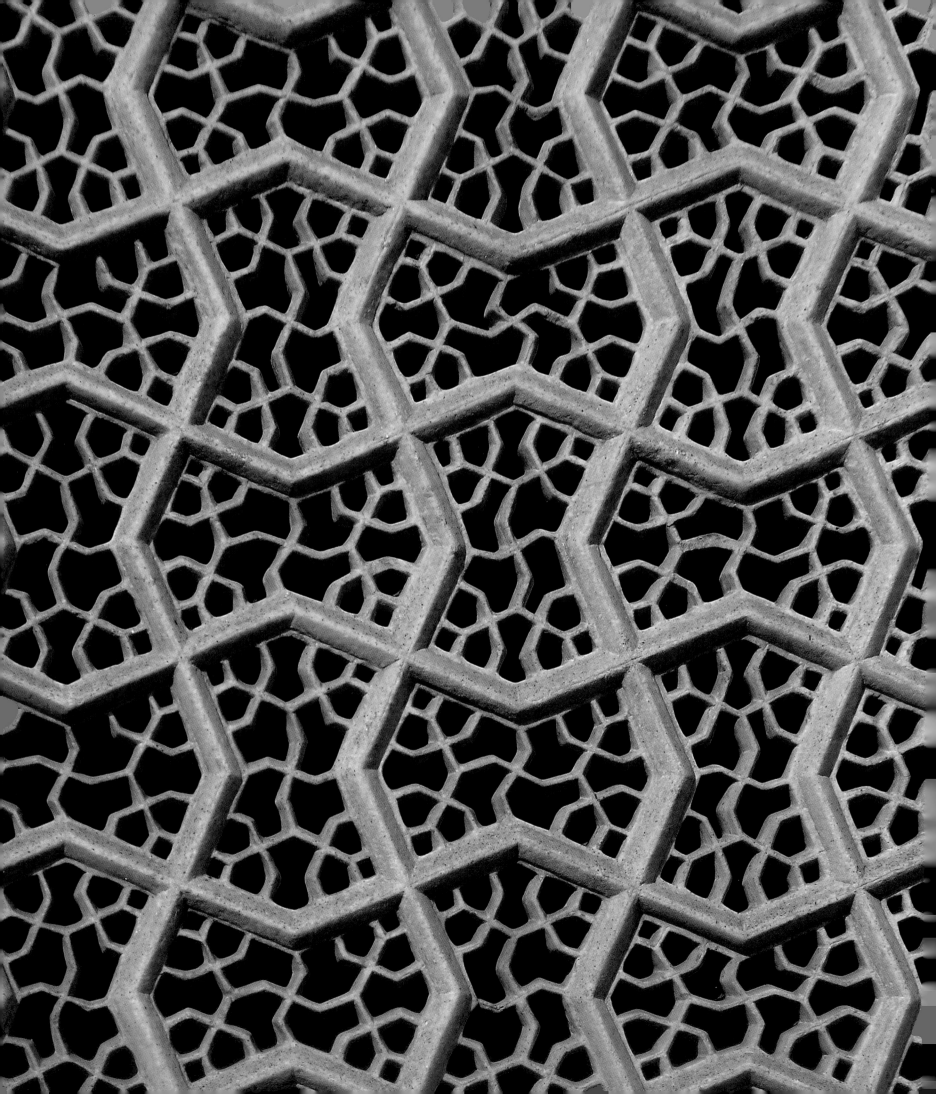

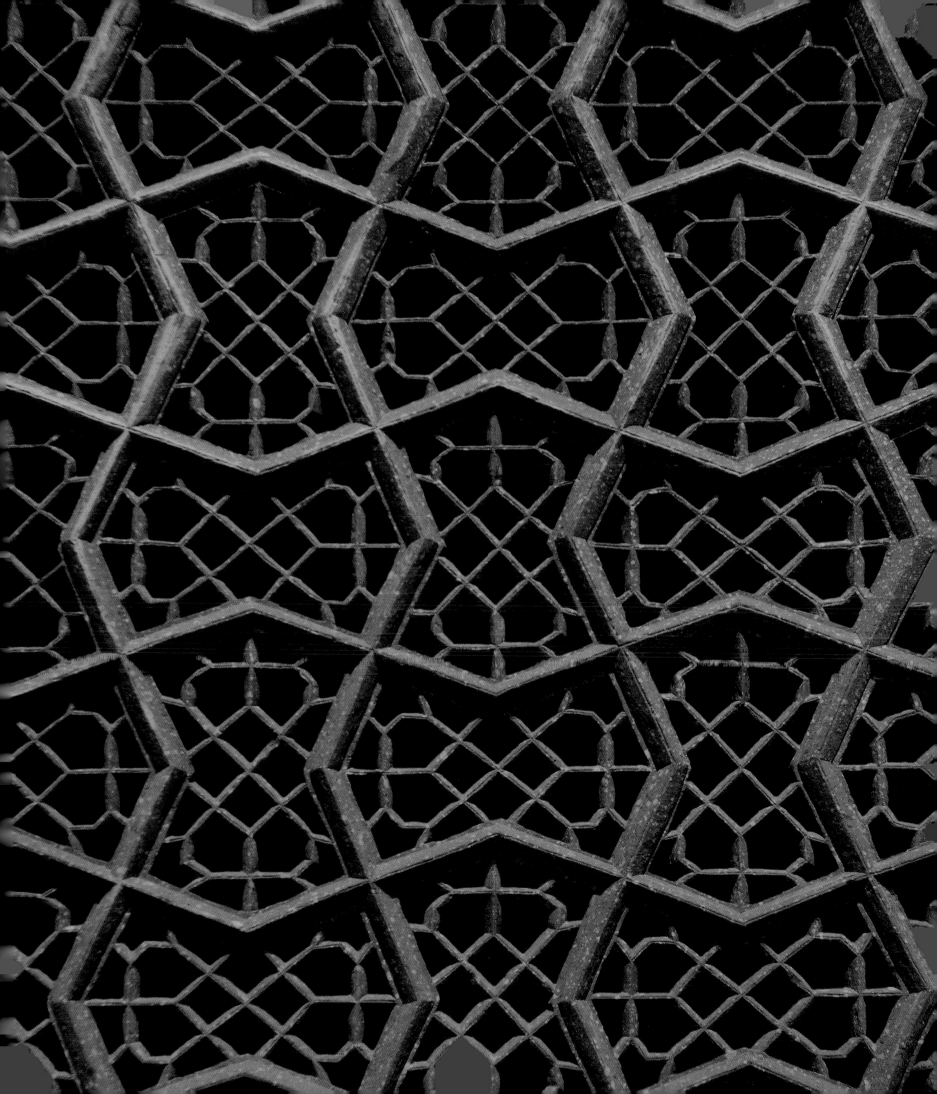

Other patterns exploit contrasts of materials and textures, such as this wall panel from inside the tomb chamber of Itimad-ad Daula (**opposite**). Here, eight-pointed stars created from two interlocking squares and filled with painted ornament are contained by uncoloured, raised bands. These bands define larger octagons, themselves containing eight-sided stars. In a coloured tiled panel from Jahangir's tomb in Lahore eight-pointed stars in red are surrounded by interlocking rings of lozenge-shaped compartments in yellow (**below**).

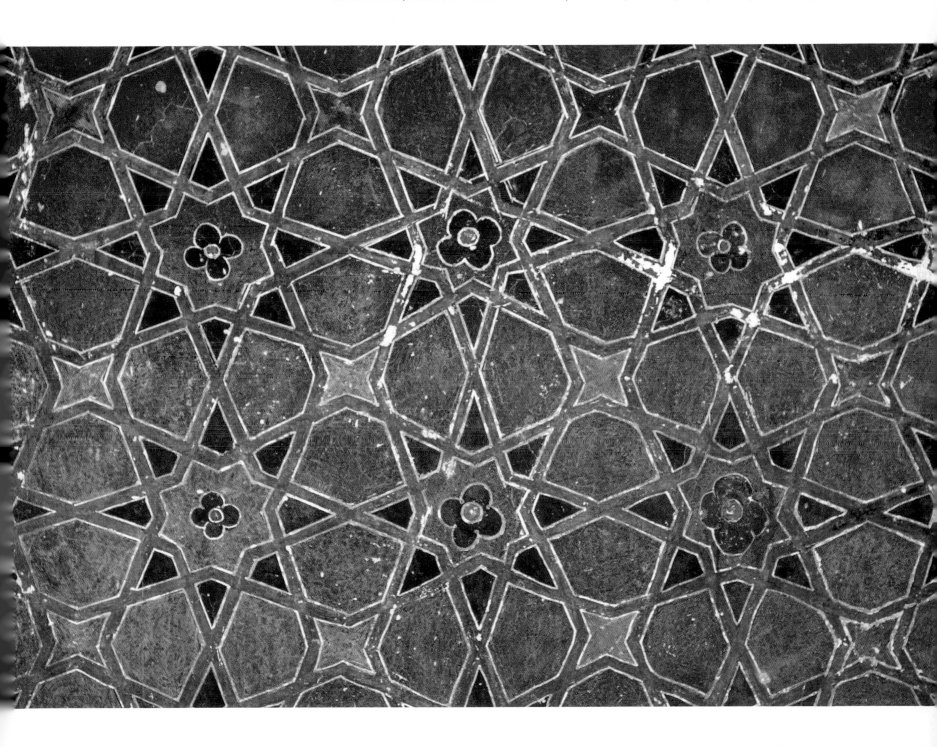

Tile mosaic panels on Lahore Fort present a catalogue of geometric patterns that must have been popular with architects that Jahangir employed when he refurbished this citadel. Contrasting yellow, blue and turquoise tiles are juxtaposed to create eight-pointed stars surrounded by interlocking rings of hexagons and five-pointed stars (**above opposite**), or rings of two-pronged, zigzag elements (**left**). Elsewhere, unglazed bricks, cut into dense foliate patterns, alternate with ceramic strips. Here too, eight-sided stars are surrounded by interlocking polygons with angled ends (**below opposite**), or six-pointed stars picked out in blue ceramic strips are separated by triple-pronged elements (**below**).

Geometry in Mughal style attains its most complicated expression in the stalactite vaults that roof entrance portals and internal domed chambers. Facets of different shapes, including lozenges composed of four or more angled sides fanning outwards from five-pointed stars, are set at angles to each other in actual three dimensions. A virtuoso demonstration of this spatial geometry is found in the tomb of Asaf Khan in Lahore (**opposite**). Here, the facets are filled with purple, yellow and white flowers on brilliant yellow, green and dark blue backgrounds, all fashioned out of glazed tile mosaic.

In other monuments in Lahore, plaster is used to achieve similar geometrical complexities, though the overall effect is less colouristic. In the stalactite vault of the tomb chamber of Jahangir the facets that surround the central star-shaped medallion are filled with painted flowers (**above**).

FOLLOWING PAGES In the Badshahi mosque the same intricate geometry is created in interlocking facets surrounding a central 16-pointed star. Here the floral decor is more precisely indicated, with flower fragments as well as sprays springing from vases.

Here an intricate, three-dimensional grid creates a
web of interlocking, lozenge-shaped facets, both
narrow and broad, with occasional eight-lobed
medallions. These elements adorn the ceiling of the
lower chamber in Itimad-ad Daula's tomb, creating
a subtle transition from the central medallion to
the walls beneath on four sides. The interiors of
the facets are filled with relief floral ornament
highlighted in gilded plaster on painted red, blue
and white backgrounds. The result is a richly textured
geometric design that serves as a gorgeously
coloured canopy for the graves beneath.

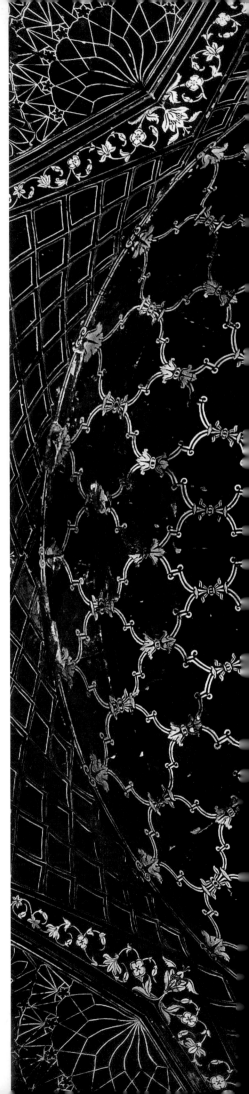

Domes provide yet further opportunities for designs with complicated geometries. A popular theme is the radiating pattern created from intersecting arcs that expand outwards from a central medallion. In the dome that roofs the principal chamber of the mosque adjacent to the Taj Mahal, these arcs are transformed into ribbon-like lattices (**opposite**).

Rather than being painted onto the dome itself, the lattices are actually cut out from the red paint of the dome to reveal the white undercoat beneath. A simpler version of this radiating design formed by crisscrossing arcs is found in the perforated circular cover of this early 17th-century *bidri* basin (**above**).
CATALOGUE 86

With their gleaming silver and brass inlays, the circular interiors of 17th-century *bidri* dishes and bowls offer ideal settings for radiating patterns capable of infinite extension. In one dish closely intersecting arcs form a central flower of great geometrical complexity which is surrounded by rings of stylized petals of ever-increasing size (**opposite**).

Another dish employs rings of chevrons, the zigzags being created out of lustrous silver on a dense black background, the angles of the chevrons opening up as they radiate outwards (**above**). Gold tints are reserved for the central medallion, which has a ring of eight tiny blossoms linked by leafy stalks.
CATALOGUE 83 & 84

Lattices composed of thin strapwork often have concave top and bottom elements, and convex side sections, that create contrasting, but harmoniously balanced interlocking curves. Identical patterns of this type are realized in white and green enamels on the curving body of this small gold jar (**opposite**), or in thin gold strips set into this dark green jade mirror-back (**left**). The lattices in both objects are filled with floral motifs, either blossoms in white enamel with spreading leaves or stylized four-lobed flowers in white jade. Both these lavishly decorated objects may be assigned to the late 17th or early 18th century. CATALOGUE 93 & 68

Moulded plaster lattices adorning the vaults and domes of the Badshahi mosque take on an almost textile quality, being treated as ribbon-like straps. Such designs are composed of interlocking figures with both straight and curved sides (**above right**). They create circles containing leafy floral motifs (**above left**). In yet more complex manifestations the straps have alternating convex and concave curves (**opposite**). Here leafy tufts mark the joints between the straps, while flowers with symmetrically arranged blossoms and leaves occupy the middle of each zone. In spite of the botanical quality of such designs, a geometric structure is always present.

The overall pattern of this sumptuous carpet dating from the 17th century has a geometric, diagonal lattice with concave and convex curves that takes on an almost vegetal quality (**opposite**). This serves as a frame for luscious blossoms and leafy stalks that trail across the brilliant red background. The lace-like tracery of the *jali* in the Khass Mahal, in the Red Fort in Delhi, employs a similar lattice with contrasting convex and concave elements, also laid out on a diagonal grid (**right**). Here, however, the floral elements are intricately cut out of white marble.
CATALOGUE 22

FOLLOWING PAGES Above the *jali* in the Khass Mahal is a semicircular panel, the interior of which is occupied by a relief representation of the scales of justice. This alludes to the righteous law dispensed throughout the Mughal empire during Shah Jahan's reign. Surrounding this allegorical motif are four full cartouches, and two half cartouches, each defined by curving and looped straps. The cartouches contain flowers with symmetrically arranged blossoms and leaves, while the spandrels above at either side are filled with floral scrolls exhibiting a similar mathematical regularity.

Arabesque

As with geometry, arabesque design in Mughal style is an artistic inheritance from the greater Islamic world. Elegant arabesque motifs were perfected in Central Asia and Persia where they were employed with considerable skill by both architects and craftsmen in the centuries prior to the Mughal period. Mughal style introduces this well evolved arabesque tradition to India, imbuing it with a local spirit through the use of indigenous materials and techniques. Mughal arabesque develops a close relationship with the world of nature, since it reconciles the mathematics of geometry with the floral decor of India. Indeed it is best considered as an abstracted naturalism, since it employs motifs inspired by actual flowers and plants, such as sinuously curved, leafy stalks and fully open, petalled blossoms. These elements, however, are combined in a distinctive unlifelike manner to create mathematically generated patterns with mirror-like or rotated symmetries, generally disposed about a central point or axis. Whatever their configuration, arabesque components are capable of infinite extension; for this reason they are ideally suited to fill panels of different shapes and awkward zones with irregular sides, such as the lozenge-shaped facets used in stalactite vaulting. Since arabesque motifs can easily be rotated, they can also serve as continuous borders, running around four sides of an architectural panel, calligraphic page or embossed metallic shield. Spiralling outwards in ever-larger arcs, arabesques can cover extensive floor areas, avoiding obstructions and filling extensions wherever required. Reduced in size and complexity, arabesque designs are suited to lobed medallions with pointed ends. They are particularly well adapted to the spandrels that serve as a transition from pointed arches to surrounding rectangular frames; in this context arabesques are often arranged symmetrically about a corner motif, angled at 45 degrees to the frame. The appearance of arabesque design in Mughal style varies from architectural detail to the decoration of manuscripts, vessels and even weapons; whatever the scale or material, it always retains a visual agility and elegance.

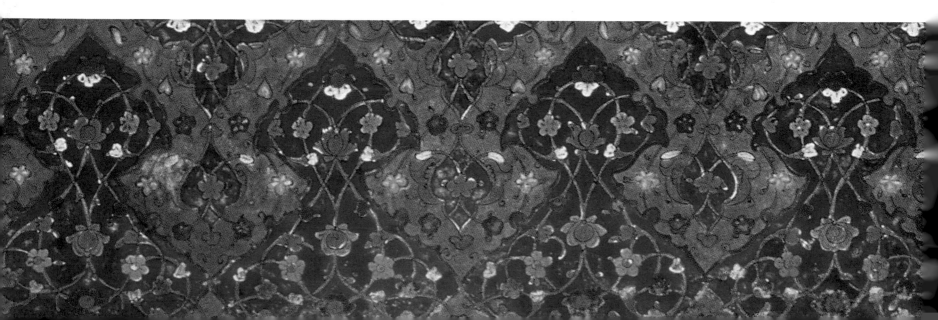

That arabesque design in Mughal style was capable of opulent expression is well illustrated in the spectacular mother-of-pearl arabesque inlays that decorate the lid of a wooden casket manufactured in a workshop in Gujarat towards the end of the 16ᵗʰ century (*see* pp. 44–45). Here supple stalks with leafy protuberances swirl outwards in perfect symmetry from a central point to fill a medallion with gently lobed sides and pointed, leafy ends. Blossoms alternating with curling leaf-like motifs achieve a consistent visual density that is a characteristic of the finest Mughal arabesque design; the same elements even extend beyond the medallion to entirely fill the rectangular lid of the casket. Throughout, the craftsman has exploited the contrast between the gleaming inlays and the dark wooden background to create a work of outstanding beauty. Another exceptional example of arabesque in Mughal style is the painted border of the Koran presented to Akbar (*below, and see* pp. 138–139). Here lines of miniature lobed cartouches in upright/upside down formation, with alternating deep blue and gold backgrounds, surround the calligraphic lines on four sides. The medallions are filled with geometrically disposed stalks with leafy protuberances, and punctuated by pink and turquoise blossoms that contrast effectively with the background colours of the lobed cartouches in which they are contained. Equally refined is the treatment of the arabesque motifs that inhabit the lobed medallions that encircle the imperial *tughra* of Shah Jahan in the middle of an illuminated page that served as an opener for an imperial album of miniature painting (*see* p. 22). Here, the overall density of arabesque ornament achieves a remarkable filigree-like effect of the greatest delicacy. The design is composed of slender tendrils, leaves and blossoms in delicate pinks and greens on contrasting and gold and blue backgrounds.

Inlaid stonework may seem at first to be an unlikely medium for the fluid curves that are the distinguishing feature of arabesque design. In the hands of expert Mughal craftsmen,

This border from a double page of a Koran dated to 1574 has intricate arabesque ornament contained in lobed cartouches with alternating gold and blue backgrounds. Miniature blossoms and leafy stalks are arranged symmetrically in accordance with a strict mathematics, demonstrating that the finest arabesque design in Mughal style is an elegant blend of floral decor and geometry. CATALOGUE 6

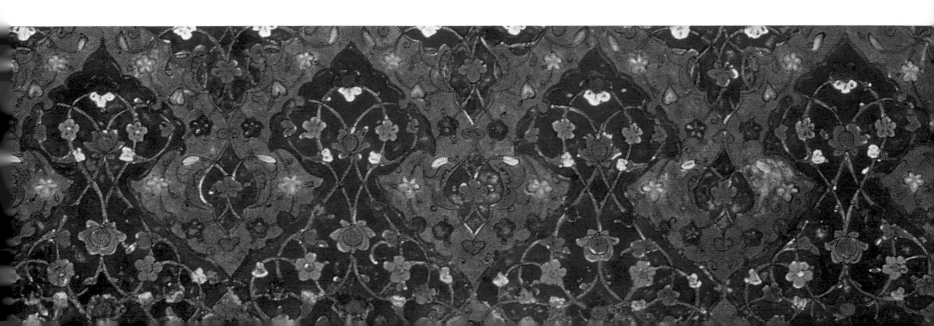

as on the tomb of Itimad-ad Daula in Agra, such motifs achieve an apparently effortless agility. Mirror and rotational symmetries govern the disposition of sinuous stalks and leafy protrusions about central blossoms that are simple, geometric figures. Highlighted in differently coloured stones set into white marble, the various arabesque components run continuously in long bands, offering a visual contrast to the more rigidly composed geometries of the wall panels which they frame. Higher up the same building, on the curving bodies of the corner rooftop minarets, lobed medallions are filled with arabesque designs that conform to a more strictly determined mathematics. Here, stalks and blossoms emanate in mirror and rotational symmetries about central flowers, themselves transformed into arabesques with four lobes, a motif that is referred to here as a quatrefoil. Arabesque design in the Taj Mahal attains a matchless perfection that is achieved through the use of thin and delicate stalk-like swirls ending in leafy extensions or blossoms. Italianate influence is detected in the stringently symmetrical arrangement of arabesque scrolls that billow outwards in almost perfectly circular arcs. The spandrels of the principal portals of the tomb, for example, have corner angled elements that resemble European lyres set at 45 degrees to the arch rather than any motif derived from the Islamic tradition! The cenotaph of Shah Jahan and its supporting podium inside the upper tomb chamber of the Taj are animated by subtly interlocking and interlacing scrolls, regularly disposed according to a subtle geometry. Throughout the monument all these arabesque components are created in superb *pietra dura* technique, with different coloured, semiprecious stones, many with smoothly curved profiles, cut into the thinnest possible pieces and set into a background of white marble.

Arabesque motifs in Mughal style sometimes combine with convoluted geometries to create intricate patterns with both angular and curved components. An example is the polychrome tile panel from the outer walls of the fort in Lahore. Here an overall geometric design is created with squares with lobed protrusions interlocking with similarly treated, smaller rectangles rotated at 45 degrees. The different zones of this complicated, mathematically determined pattern are crowded with arabesque motifs. These exhibit curling stems and leafy protrusions scrolling outward from repeated, central quatrefoil medallions so as to achieve a remarkable visual density. Only by the use of tiles with strongly contrasting colours can the different components of the design be visually distinguished. Another instance of this combination of complex geometries with arabesque motifs is found in the faceted vaults and domes that roof external porches and interior chambers, as in the side niches of the antechamber of Akbar's tomb at Sikandra. Here, a star-shaped medallion is surrounded by a network of four-sided, lozenge-shaped facets. These facets are set at angles to each other three dimensionally, so as to extend all the way to the supporting walls beneath. The different shaped compartments are all filled with arabesques that have symmetrically disposed blossoms and trailing stems with leafy protrusions. The motifs are realized in intricately worked moulded plaster and then gilded, thereby differentiating them from their brightly coloured backgrounds. A more brilliant demonstration of the ability of arabesque patterns to occupy irregular shaped compartments can hardly be imagined. This device of filling mathematically determined stalactite facets with 'tufts' of moulded arabesque is, in fact, a persistent feature in Mughal architecture. Deriving from Central Asia and Persia where this practice was well developed, stalactites decorated with arabesque ornament appear in the plasterwork that roofs vaulted chambers and domes; on occasion the same motifs are realized in marble worked in delicate relief.

Not all arabesque design in Mughal style conforms to such mathematical rigour. When painted onto a textile, for instance, it sometimes achieves a greater freedom, with curving stalks and leafy ends combining together in a more sinuous and relaxed manner, unrestrained by compartments, but nonetheless visually compact. Here, again, colour is employed to visually distinguish the different interlocking elements. The same is true of the murals with which some Mughal monuments are adorned. Those of Itimad-ad Daula's tomb, for instance, have painted panels with quatrefoils disposed on a geometric grid to fill the spaces. These are interspersed with leafy arabesque arcs angled at 45 degrees which maintain the overall geometric structure. When applied at a smaller scale to metal or jade objects Mughal arabesque design inevitably takes on a harder, more controlled quality, but does not lose its essential flexibility. Brass strips inlaid into the sides of a silver ewer create elegantly interlocking arabesque scrolls that emanate outwards in elliptical arcs from central blossoms so as to perfectly fit the curving sides of the vessel. The elements all end in symmetrically disposed curling leaves so as to achieve the desired harmonious effect. A similar concern with overall symmetry is seen in the gold strips set into a tiny jade box that curve gracefully outwards from a central quatrefoil medallion.

Arabesque design in Mughal times must have been considered protective since it was often used to embellish instruments of war. Metallic shields of different shapes as well as arm- and chest-guards are decorated with arabesque motifs, either by embossing, in which the swirling arcs are raised above the plane of the metallic background, or by the repoussé technique, by which brightly coloured brass strips are hammered into a grey metallic background to create the required pattern. Curving loops of leafy stalks terminating in miniature buds are arranged around a central flower so as to fill the central panel of a rectangular chest-guard; alternatively, in a tapering arm-guard with a pointed end, the stalks radiate outwards in regular arcs from one or more central quatrefoil. In spite of their metallic composition these patterns exhibit a graceful elegance, best appreciated in the spreading, supple curves of the arabesque. Such designs are invariably dictated by a geometric structure, though, as in all of the finest examples of arabesque in Mughal style, this never hinders the effortless fluidity of their curving components.

Bands of arabesque ornament framing the outer wall panels on the tomb of Itimad-ad Daula are combined in rotational symmetry, with identical patterns appearing in alternating, upright/upside down formation. Stalks with leafy terminations looping in different directions emanate from central multi-lobed blossoms. Rare, fossilized stones with contrasting colours and textures, set into white marble, help distinguish the different swirling stalks and curling leaves, all of which are mathematically dictated.

Richer, more complex arabesque designs adorn the circular shafts of the corner minarets that rise above the rooftop of Itimad-ad Daula's tomb. Tightly contained in elliptical cartouches with gently lobed sides and pointed tops and bottoms, arabesque designs swell outwards from central quatrefoils (**opposite**). The quatrefoils are in themselves combinations of blossoms with leafy protuberances, linked by swirls of leafy stalks. Each blossom conforms to a symmetrical structure that integrates stylized leafy cores with lobed frames, all of the elements being distinguished by different coloured stones (**left**).

FOLLOWING PAGES Arabesque design is capable of being enlarged or contracted; and for this reason it is ideally suited to fill the spandrels above the arches of monumental portals or of arched doorways and wall niches. The gateway to Akbar's tomb at Sikandra, for example, has spandrels filled with symmetrically disposed motifs set at 45 degrees to the outer frame (**left**). The flowing scrolls and medallion-like blossoms are realized by white marble inlays set into a black stone background. A similar effect is achieved in moulded red sandstone in the spandrels above the arched windows of Itimad-ad Daula's tomb (**right**).

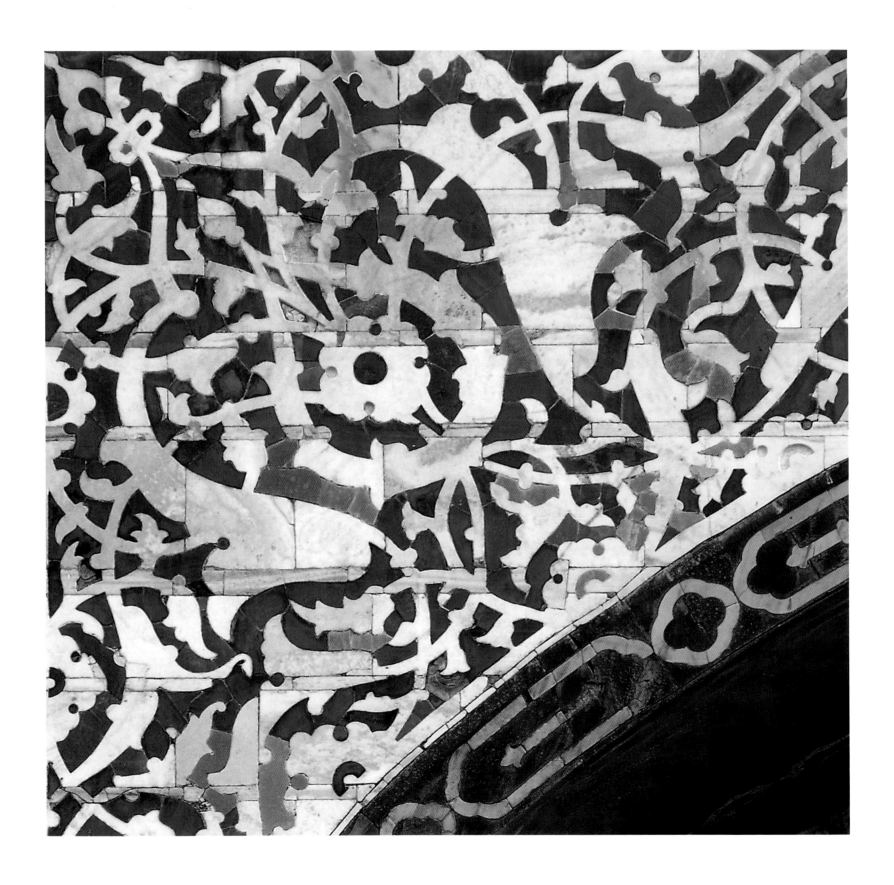

Arabesque design in Mughal style finds its purest expression in the Taj Mahal. Nowhere is this better seen than in the treatment of the spandrels above the arches that frame the axial portals of the domed tomb (**opposite**). Here, angled Italianate styled, lyre-like elements occupy the corners, from which leafy scrolls emanate in regular formation on either side. These arabesque elements are all created in the finest *pietra dura*. Similar lyre-shaped motifs appear elsewhere in Shah Jahan's architecture, as in this corner detail from a *jali* in the Khass Mahal in the Red Fort in Delhi (**below**).

The white marble cenotaphs of Mumtaz Mahal and Shah Jahan in the upper tomb chamber of the Taj Mahal are enhanced by superb *pietra dura* decoration. The emperor's tomb is adorned with arabesque designs, including a floral roundel surrounded by arabesque curves, with angled lyre-like elements at the corners (**opposite**). Elsewhere, *pietra dura* borders with continuous arabesque motifs frame wall panels with relief carvings (**left**). Here stalk-like arcs in heart-shaped formation have stylized blossoms aligned along the middle of the bands; flowers with fringed petals mark the termination of the arcs.

Coloured tile mosaic, though a laborious medium, offers opportunities to create geometric and arabesque patterns of mathematical complexity and colouristic brilliance. This is well illustrated in the panels that adorn the outer walls of Lahore Fort. In this example, stars with four- or eight-lobed points tightly interlock with angled rectangles with pointed sides and ends. The stars and rectangles are both filled with tightly composed quatrefoil arabesque motifs in dark blue and green tones that stand out from the bright yellow background.

When realized in the painted medium, as in this border from an early 17th-century cotton floorspread, Mughal arabesque takes on a less geometrically determined quality (**detail above**). Here, deep reds and greens are used to create multi-lobed cartouches filled with stylized blossoms disposed in reverse symmetry. The intervening spaces are occupied by swirling leafy scrolls picked out in white. The overall effect of visual compactness serves as an effective contrast to the central panel, which portrays a flowering plant on a white background (*see* p. 190-191). CATALOGUE 26

FOLLOWING PAGES Painted arabesque motifs are also found in Mughal architecture, as in this wall panel from the interior of Akbar's tomb in Sikandra. Here the principal motif, with regularly arranged quadruple lobes painted in gold, contains blossoms with feathery blue petals and red cores. The quatrefoils are laid out on a geometric grid that extends both horizontally and vertically. The spaces in between are filled with arcs with leafy ends angled in perfect rotational symmetry. Such a mathematically determined design is integrated into the overall decor of the monument.

Arabesque swirls created in silver and brass in the inlaid *bidri* technique create an uninterrupted design that covers the tapering body of this elegant, 17th-century ewer (**opposite**). Arabesque arcs expand outwards from small, centrally placed six-petalled flowers, eventually terminating in curling leaves or five-petalled flowers. At a smaller scale is this tiny green jade box dating from the 18th century decorated with arabesque curves in thin gold strips (**right**). Straight 'stalks' with blossoms emanate in four directions from a central quatrefoil. CATALOGUE 79 & 66

Arabesque designs enhance both these examples of armour dating from the 17th and early 18th century. The tapering *bazuband*, or arm-guard, has arabesque arcs flanking a vertical axis (**right**). Created in inlaid brass, the swirls are ingeniously fitted into the tapering body and pointed tip of the guard. In the body-guard (**opposite**), embossed arabesque motifs flow outwards in regular formation from a small central flower, so as to entirely fill the rectangular panel. The surrounding frame has foliate ornament in beaten gold. The hinges are for leather bands to secure the metal guard to the chest of the warrior.
CATALOGUE 99 & 98

FOLLOWING PAGES The half-dome over one of the side niches in the antechamber of Akbar's tomb has a star-shaped medallion filled with stylized floral ornament that almost approaches an arabesque in its geometricized forms. Genuine arabesques inhabit the surrounding interlocking, lozenge-shaped facets. The arabesque motifs are created in plaster relief and gilded, so as to distinguish them from the brightly painted blue and white backgrounds. Their expanding swirling leafy stalks fill the facets, set at angles to each other, so as to achieve a transition from the central medallion to the walls beneath.

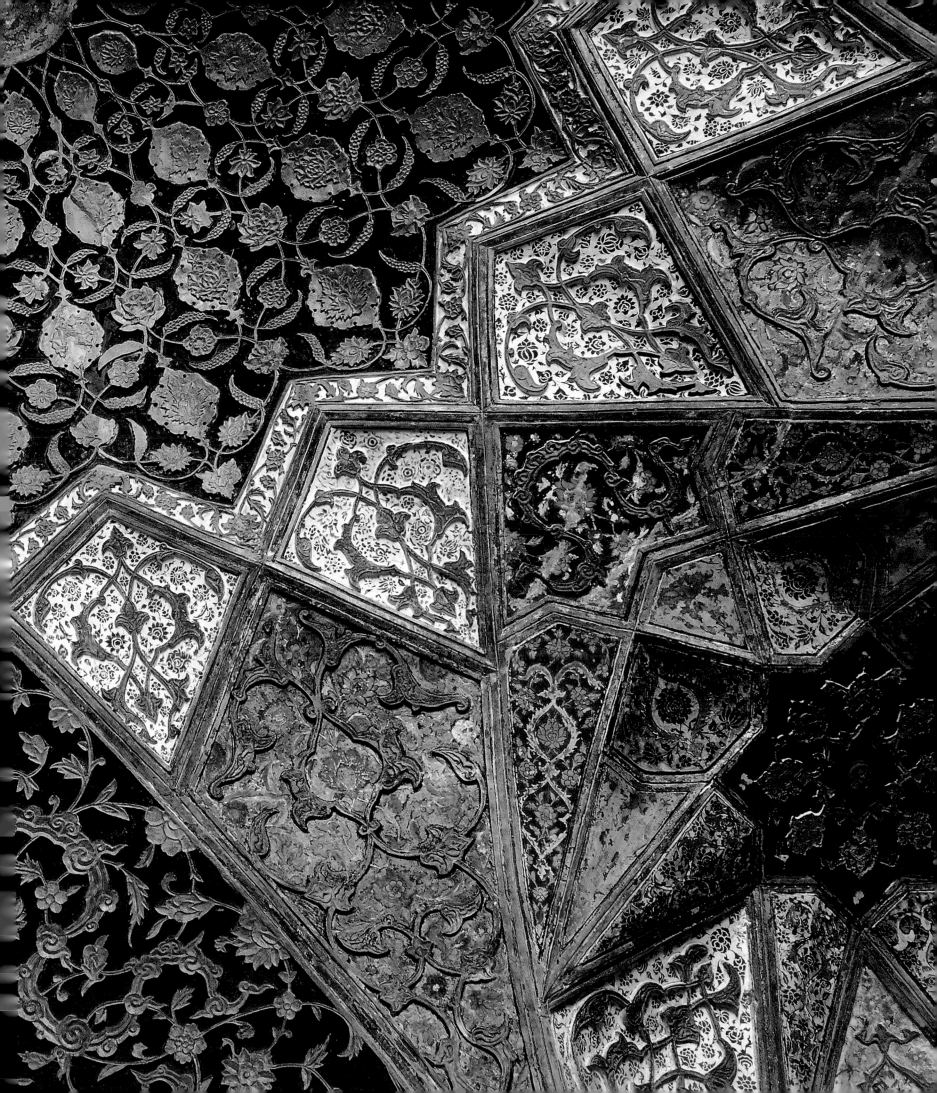

CALLIGRAPHY

Of all the decorative arts embraced by Mughal style, calligraphy enjoyed the highest reputation at the imperial court. The Mughal emperors were great bibliophiles, beginning with Babur, founder of the dynasty, who in 1526 transported his personal library from Uzbekistan to northern India on his heroic conquering campaign. Though his grandson Akbar is supposed to have had difficulty in reading, his *kitabkhana* numbered many thousands of volumes, all of which were catalogued and valued. The collection included works in Turkish, Persian and Arabic, as well as in Indian languages, and covered a wide range of subjects, from religion and philosophy, to history and science, and poetry and epic literature. Many of these works dated back to pre-Mughal times, and doubtless served as models for the calligraphers employed at the Mughal court. The books created anew for Akbar and his successors involved the skills of translators, calligraphers, illuminators and painters. But according to Akbar's great confidant, adviser and biographer, Abu'l Fazl, calligraphy was considered a higher art than illumination and painting. Abu'l Fazl defined the principal calligraphic styles current in India as well as in contemporary Persia, categorizing them according to the proportion of straight and round letters. At the top of this calligraphic hierarchy, in his opinion, was *nasta`liq*, since it was formed entirely of rounded letters; certainly it was one of the most popular scripts with Mughal calligraphers, used widely in architecture, manuscripts and the fine arts.

In addition to describing the various calligraphic styles, Abu'l Fazl also gives the names of the most distinguished calligraphers in the Mughal *kitabkhana*, tracing their lineages and styles back to celebrated practitioners who had worked in earlier times in Central Asia and Persia. That calligraphy in Mughal India continued to be closely linked with figures of this tradition is hardly surprising considering the number of experts who emigrated from Persia, and whose signatures are often recorded on the manuscripts and monuments that they worked on. While the

Mughal emperors are well known to have been keen appraisers of the miniature paintings produced in the imperial *kitabkhanas*, they also had an experienced eye for calligraphy, recording their judgements in the margins of the various pages. Such memos suggest that the emperors tended to place more value on works by Persian specialists than their Indian counterparts. Perhaps for this reason it is the Persian manner that tends to govern the forms of calligraphy in Mughal style, even when realized in characteristic Indian materials, techniques and colour schemes.

This merging of imported and indigenous traditions is best illustrated in the magnificent Koran transcribed by the calligrapher Hibatallah al-Husayni, and presented to Akbar in Lahore. This single-volume work repeats the format, decorative illumination and calligraphic styles perfected in 15ᵗʰ-century Persia. Even so, the arabesque details with bright pink, orange and green colouristic flourishes on more conventional blue, gold and white backgrounds indicate that this Koran could only have been produced in a Mughal *kitabkhana*. Apart from its extravagant decoration, the text is a virtuoso exhibition of the calligrapher's art, with varying styles of letters in different sizes combined on a single page so as to divide the text into more readable portions, and to highlight the headings of the successive chapters. Such a display of diverse scripts was employed by calligraphers to advertise their abilities, thereby attracting royal admiration and, hopefully, patronage.

Koranic quotations in Mughal art are by no means confined to manuscript pages. Mosques and tombs were embellished with panels of Arabic texts, most often in *naskh* and *thuluth*. With their clear contrasts of curves and verticals, these scripts were ideally suited to public, large-scale settings, in spite of the fact that the obviously cursive style of their letters was difficult to reproduce in masonry. A fine example of monumental *naskh* is seen in the Jami

This Koranic passage runs in a band across the top of the central *mihrab* within the prayer chamber of the Jami mosque at Fatehpur Sikri. It is written in *naskh* script, the letters of which display slender elongated tails. Though carved in shallow relief out of sandstone and then gilded on a dark blue background, the inscription retains its essentially hand-written, calligraphic quality.

mosque at Fatehpur Sikri, where the central *mihrab* in the rear wall of the prayer chamber is surrounded by a band of exactly this type of script. Another stylish set of *naskh* texts is found in the series of eight panels adorning the corridor of the tomb of Shaykh Salim Chishti that stands in the courtyard of this same mosque. Here single-line quotations with gracefully formed and generously spaced letters are created in sharp relief, the background being cut away so as to emphasize the different curves and vertical strokes of the letters, divided by a single, bold horizontal stroke. Other refined examples of relief calligraphy are the royal titles of Jahangir cut into the sides of the green marble throne within the Red Fort at Agra. Here the letters in *nasta`liq* script are elegantly disposed so as to fill the lobed cartouches in which they are contained.

It is, however, in the Taj Mahal that Mughal monumental calligraphy assumes its most grandiose expression, here executed in matchless *pietra dura* technique, with *thuluth* letters fashioned out of black stone pieces set into a white marble background. It has been estimated that there are almost 1,000 metres of Koranic inscriptions on the Taj, arranged in frames around the external portals and interior doorways of the main tomb, as well as on the adjacent mosque and the entrance gateway to the great *char-bagh* garden. They were all designed by 'Amanat Khan, an eminent calligrapher who had come to India from Shiraz in Persia, and who did not hesitate to leave his signature. His inscriptions occupy the full width of architectural bands, and employ transverse strokes that provide a welcome visual contrast to the curving contours and elongated vertical tails of the letters themselves. The passages speak of the Day of Judgement and of the paradise guaranteed to the faithful – surely an appropriate theme for a monument intended to perpetuate Shah Jahan's memory of his beloved queen. Smaller, but equally fine *pietra dura* inscriptions in *naskh* adorn the upper cenotaph of Mumtaz Mahal within the tomb chamber of the Taj. They too quote passages from the Koran mentioning the promise of paradise. That such calligraphic quotations in religious architecture are not exclusively restricted to stonework is demonstrated by the tile mosaic panels of the mosque of Wazir Khan in Lahore. Here letters in contrasting *nasta`liq* and *thuluth* style are laboriously cut out of bright blue tiles and set into brilliant white and yellow tiled backgrounds so as to create a polychrome calligraphy that is considered unrivalled in all of Mughal style.

If *thuluth* and *naskh* are the preferred styles of calligraphy at an architectural scale it is *nasta`liq* that most often prevails in smaller works of art, especially in the metalwork and manuscript pages produced in the Mughal *kitabkhanas* and *karkhanas*. Koranic passages were believed to be magically protective, which explains their appearance on the arms of the period, such as the swords and bows embellished with gold letters, beaten into steel blades by the painstaking process of damascening. Such auspicious weapons were often made for the Mughal emperors, as well as for other rulers of the period, who are named in the inscriptions. Other metal objects were also sometimes vehicles of calligraphic art. One cast-brass vase has regularly spaced, engraved cartouches with tightly composed arabesque designs alternating with inscriptions in compressed *naskh*, the letters of which are sharply incised and set against a hatched ground filled with contrasting black paste. A comparable object is a circular silver dish with three concentric rings of text that encircle the name of Allah in the middle. Though the letters here are incised in comparatively shallow relief, they create a text that can be read continuously around the circular surface.

Even on a tiny scale, calligraphic metalwork has a contribution to make to Mughal style, as is evident in the exquisitely cast gold coins known as *mohurs*, with texts often designed by the leading calligraphers of the day. The *mohurs* issued during Jahangir's reign generally have one side inscribed with the Kalima, or Profession of Faith, and the date and place where the coin was minted; the other side gives the emperor's name, titles and regnal year. The swelling strokes of the letters that sweep boldly across the diameters of the finest of Jahangir's coins contrast with delicate scrolls of foliation that appear in the background. Compositions with flowing *nasta`liq* script in circular frames are sometimes also executed in opaque watercolour, as in the illuminated page with a central *tughra*, or ornamental calligraphic signature, giving the name and titles of Shah Jahan. This painted medallion, filled with interlocking and looped letters, served as a focal point for concentric rings of gold and blue lobed cartouches containing intricate arabesque scrolls. This splendidly decorated page served as an opener for an album of exquisite miniature paintings specially assembled for the emperor himself.

Further contrasts of letters with shorter and longer sweeping tails written in *nasta`liq* script are to be found in the *qit`as*, or pages intended to advertise the talents of the calligraphers. Such pages were much admired by the Mughal emperors who had them bound in special albums. Here the calligraphers tended to transcribe a few select lines of Persian poetry in black ink on a white or coloured background, so as to direct attention to the graceful curved contours of the letters themselves. Sometimes the quotations are arranged in blocks of two or three lines of text set at 45 degrees to the frame of the page, as if to remind the viewer that it is the writing itself that is the principal object of interest, not the literary content of the lines. The spaces between the letters are generally filled with floral ornament that enhances the calligraphy, but is always visually subservient to it. A further example of display calligraphy in *nasta`liq* script, partly arranged in angled panels, is found on one of the most truly spectacular objects of the Mughal era. This is a wooden box entirely covered with minute ivory and mother-of-pearl inlays, most of them arranged as compact lines of Arabic and Persian poetry. The letters have a fluidity and elegance that rival the finest lines of calligraphy executed in ink. The verses are framed by floral ornament with scrolling stalks and curving leaves, which are trademarks of the workshops in Gujarat where this object was fashioned.

PRECEDING PAGES This double page with verses from Suras 18 and 19 comes from a Koran presented to Akbar in 1574. The manuscript is a display piece of calligraphic art: three lines of larger *muhaqqaq* script on white backgrounds frame three blocks, each with seven lines of smaller *naskh* script on gold backgrounds; chapter headings in black *riqa'* script, such as that at the top of the right-hand page, are in black on a gold background. The different scripts are unified by the intricate arabesque border. CATALOGUE 6

This calligraphic panel is one of eight set into the walls of the corridor that surrounds the mausoleum of Shaykh Salim Chishti in the courtyard of the Jami mosque at Fatehpur Sikri (**below**). It reads: 'In the name of God, the merciful and the compassionate.' The script is *naskh*, the letters being painted in gold, and set against a background cut out of white marble and painted deep blue. The clearly defined curves and verticals of the script are relieved by a floral scroll that weaves its way behind the letters.

Panels of flowing *nasta`liq* script spell out an invocation (**below**) and the name of Prince Salim, the future Emperor Jahangir (**opposite**). These are incised in deep relief onto the sides of the green marble throne that stands on the terrace in front of the Diwan-i Khass in the Red Fort at Agra. The letters are arranged within lobed cartouches, and enhanced by a leafy scroll behind the diacritical marks. This floral decor is also continued in the relief arabesque ornament that appears on either side.

The cenotaph of Mumtaz Mahal in the upper tomb chamber of the Taj Mahal is adorned with arabesque and floral ornament executed in the finest *pietra dura* manner. The *naskh* inscription at the top of the cenotaph quotes paradisiacal passages from the Koran, similar to those on the outer portals of the monument (*see* pp. 160—161). They suggest a foretaste of Mumtaz's eternal residence in paradise. The *naskh* inscription on the base of the cenotaph serves as the epitaph of Mumtaz; it gives 1631 as the date of her death.

FOLLOWING PAGES Religious inscriptions in cut-out, luminous blue tiles fill the arched panels on the walls of the prayer chamber, courtyard and entrance gateway of Wazir Khan's mosque in Lahore. In the panel on the left, the spaces between the curving letters of flowing *nasta`liq* script are filled with blossoms on a white background; the panel on the right employs a compressed version of *thuluth* script, with hardly any gaps between the letters. The *thuluth* script, with characteristic extended vertical tails, is set onto a sparkling yellow background.

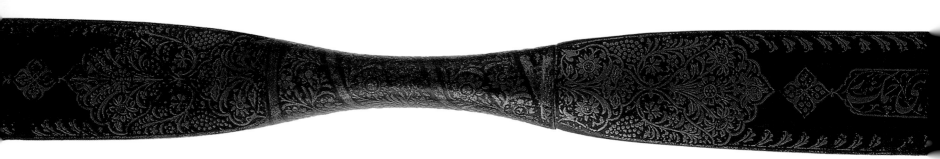

Inscriptions in gold worked meticulously into the steel blades of weapons illustrate the magically protective properties of calligraphy in Mughal times. The sword of Tipu Sultan, the late 18th-century ruler of Karnataka, is modelled closely on earlier Mughal weapons **(top)**. It bears a Koranic passage in *naskh* script. In contrast, the flank of the bow that once belonged to Bahadur Shah Zafar II, the last Mughal emperor, is inscribed with his personal name and an Urdu couplet, both in *nasta`liq* script **(above)**.
CATALOGUE 95 & 100

The engraved *naskh* inscriptions on this late 16th-
century, cast-brass bowl bear invocations to the Five
Members of the House of the Prophet, that are
typical of Shi`a Islamic piety and devotion (**right**). The
calligraphic panels contained in lobed cartouches
alternate with eight-pointed stars filled with
quatrefoil arabesque motifs. In the copper dish
dating from the late 18th century the calligraphy is
arranged in three concentric rings around a
medallion with the name of Allah in the middle
(**opposite**). The inner circle in *naskh* script gives the
names of Allah, Muhammad and Ali. Koranic
passages fill the outer circles. CATALOGUE 76 & 85

These two gold *mohurs* of Jahangir (obverse and
reverse shown for each coin), issued in Agra, dated
1608 (**opposite above**) and 1619 (**opposite below**) have
lines of *nasta`liq* script giving the title and regnal
year of the emperor. The sweeping horizontal tails of
the letters flowing across the coins contrast with the
floral scrolls in the background. A similarly dexterous
arrangement of letters within a circular frame is also
found in this painted composition from a *shamsa*
that serves as the centrepiece of an opening page
to a mid-17th-century album of Shah Jahan (**right**).
Here the letters are in *tughra* form, with interlocking,
looped tails. CATALOGUE 74, 75 & 1

The page of 17ᵗʰ-century calligraphy presents extracts from the *Munajat-i Hazrat Ali*, a collection of prayers dating from pre-Mughal times (**opposite**). Double lines of *nasta`liq* script, in contrasting larger and smaller sizes on differently coloured backgrounds, are organized in horizontal and diagonal blocks so as to direct the attention of the viewer to the abilities of the calligrapher. The panels of script alternating with panels of floral and arabesque ornament are surrounded by a border depicting a delicately painted, monochrome forest landscape. CATALOGUE 2

Display pages known as *qit`as* were popular with Mughal calligraphers as vehicles of their skills in handling different scripts (**right & left**). These three examples dating from the mid-16ᵗʰ century to the early 18ᵗʰ century, all in *nasta`liq* script, present lines of Persian poetry. The literary value of the quotations, however, is of secondary importance to the actual style of the letters themselves, either angled on the page, or set in compartments and borders, and enhanced by colourful floral backgrounds and frames (*see also* pp. 210—211). CATALOGUE 3, 5 & 4

This wooden chest accommodated instruments of the calligrapher's profession: reed pens, fine knives, inks, and a wooden block for trimming pens. Its densely packed mother-of-pearl calligraphic inlays in *nasta`liq* script give the name of its maker, Shaykh Muhammad Munshi Ghaznavi, and 1587 as the date of its manufacture. The script also quotes verses of Persian poetry, including lines penned by the celebrated Sufi mystic Jalal al-Din Rumi that link the calligrapher to his imagined lover, thereby imbuing the box with a romantic literary spirit. CATALOGUE 14

FOLLOWING PAGES This majestic *thuluth* inscription from Sura 36 of the Koran runs continuously along three sides of the broad frame that defines the arched portal on the east face of the Taj Mahal. The letters have characteristic curving profiles and elongated tails, through which runs a central band, all realized in superb black stone inlays set into a white marble background. Like the other grandly scaled calligraphic compositions on the monument, designed by 'Amanat Khan and dated between 1632 and 1643, this passage emphasizes the Day of Judgement and the promise of paradise to the faithful.

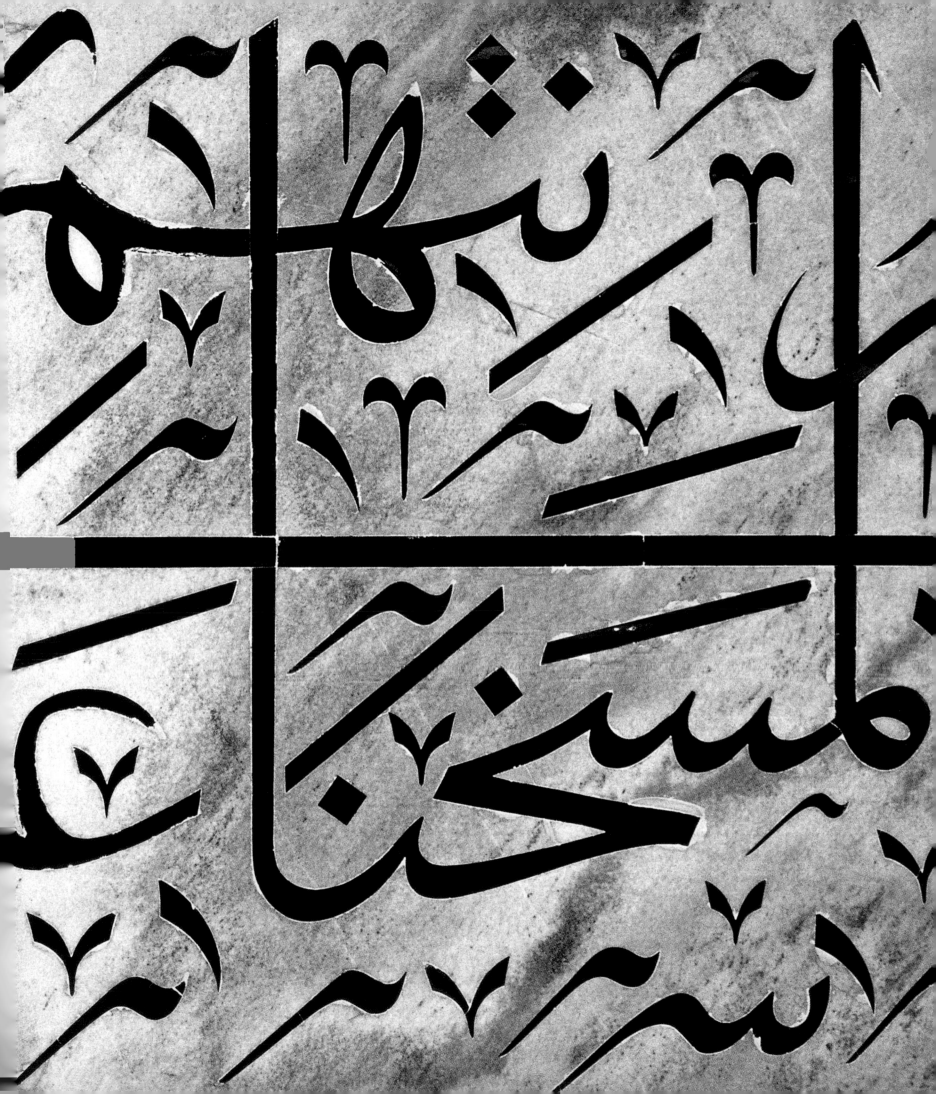

FLOWERS

Flowers constituted the most common and best loved decorative element in every sphere of Mughal style – from architectural ornament to the adornment of utilitarian objects. Whatever the scale at which they worked, and whatever the material they used, Mughal artists evidently made every effort to create an all-encompassing floral environment. This enhanced both the public and private zones of the emperor and his nobles, from the architectural settings in which they conducted their everyday business of state or enjoyed their more discreet pleasures, to the carpets and textiles with which they adorned their tents, audience halls and private apartments, to the costumes, jewels and weapons that they wore, to the dishes that they ate off, the cups from which they sipped their wine or the *huqqa* bowls that held their tobacco, and even the writing boxes in which they stored pens to sign their imperial edicts. Underpinning this deeply felt attraction for flowers was the notion of paradise as a garden, stocked with wondrous plants and fruits. While the Mughals inherited the idea of a paradisiacal garden from traditional Islamic teaching, they nonetheless took greater pains than any of their predecessors or contemporaries to realize this concept in their everyday lives. As an inscription in the Diwan-i Khass in the Red Fort in Delhi proclaims: "If there be paradise on earth, it is here, it is here, it is here!" So as to remind Shah Jahan and his courtiers that no such paradise could be complete without flowers and flowing water, the nearby Rang Mahal has a magnificent lotus fountain sculpted out of the marble floor (*see* p. 280).

Many Mughal emperors took interest in flowers as part of their overall delight in the natural world. Babur described the different plants that he observed after he conquered India, while Jahangir ordered 'portraits' of particular flowers, and laid out gardens where such flowers might flourish, especially in the valley of Kashmir where the climate was wetter and cooler. In spite of their fascination with India's indigenous flora the Mughals always retained a certain botanical yearning for their lost Central Asian homeland: how else to explain the

appearance in Mughal architecture and art of flowers such as the poppy, carnation and tulip that were then unknown in the plains of India? From this point of view Mughal floral decor was inspired by the plants derived from the lands of the Islamic world, as represented in woven carpets, carved jades and the painted margins of manuscripts. However, they did not hesitate to augment this imported floral decor with native species. Not only did the artists who created Mughal style introduce flowers such as the lotus and the lily, they never lost sight of India's long-standing tradition of imbuing flowers and plants with magical, medicinal and mythological properties, as realized in the religious legends and monuments of Buddhism and Hinduism.

In spite of their knowledge of the different varieties of flowers, whether derived from Central Asia or native to India, the Mughals were not always concerned with botanical accuracy. Their aim seems to have been to create an overall floral milieu rather than a record of precisely rendered, actual plants. For this reason it is sometimes difficult to identify the particular flowers that are represented in marble reliefs, woven textiles or inlaid metal bowls since the natural forms in these and other comparable contexts are often subtly altered: petals and stamens are multiplied to present visually balanced compositions; blossoms are arranged in symmetrical, but unlifelike formations. In the end, however, such departures never detract from an overall appreciation of nature; to the contrary, buildings or works of art embellished in this somewhat inaccurate manner nonetheless manage to suggest an actual garden planted with assorted flowers.

Naturalistic and quasi-naturalistic floral motifs are found side by side in Mughal style, as in the red sandstone walls of tombs and palaces. The gateway to Akbar's tomb at Sikandra, for instance, is adorned with panels of magnificent, though obviously stylized white marble blossoms that seem to cloak the monument like a flowered shawl. More realistic are the

Lines of flowers serve as ideal borders for this small Ivory box (**opposite**) and cotton *patka* or waist-sash (**below**). The flowers carved in relief show Irises and a variety of rich open blossoms arranged symmetrically around a central tulip-like bloom. The flowers printed onto the cloth represent more natural, brilliant red carnations, repeated in an unlifelike manner that is typical of Mughal style. CATALOGUE 71 & 30

panels depicting fruits on the Turkish sultana's house at Fatehpur Sikri, and irises and lilies on the mosque adjacent to the Taj Mahal in Agra. In both these instances the relief carving perfectly captures the forms of different fruits and the twirling petals and stamens and curling leaves of actual flowers, even if these are combined in unlifelike symmetrical formations. This mixture of realism and artificiality can also be observed in the white marble panels on the Taj Mahal, especially in the majestic bunches of flowers that spring forth from fanciful vases carved onto the interior walls of the tomb chamber. Even when realized in the demanding technique of *pietra dura*, as on the *jali* screens that surround the cenotaphs of Shah Jahan and Mumtaz Mahal, the flowers appear to be depicted with convincing realism. Only on closer inspection can it be observed that the combinations of petals, stamens and leaves, while recalling actual flowers, are not necessarily botanically truthful. However, as has already been noticed, this was never a major preoccupation of Mughal artists; rather, it was the creation of a floral decor that would suggest a paradisiacal garden.

When created in variant materials, such as mirror pieces set into plaster, tile mosaic or gold paint on plaster, flowers in Mughal architecture become even less lifelike, though this loss of naturalism is compensated for by the reflecting textures and brilliantly gleaming colours. This is well seen in the flowers-in-vase motif that was imported by the Mughals from Central Asia and Persia, but which gained great popularity in India, partly because it accorded with the indigenous pot-and-foliage motif that dates back to well before the Mughal era. Vases with flowers are also found in the decorative arts, as in the cotton hangings and floor cloths displaying brilliant contrasts of red and white. A related topic is the single flower with symmetrically arranged blossoms within an arched niche. This occurs in buildings, as in the embossed brass doors of the Bibi-ka Maqbara in Aurangabad as well as in cotton and velvet hangings. Also to be found in the printed and woven textiles of the period are flowers arranged in long rows. Lines of flowers of different types, sometimes combined together, adorn velvet cushions, brocaded hangings and printed cotton *patkas*. While the rhythmic repetition of these motifs lends an inevitable artificiality to this floral decor, the individual flowers are often depicted realistically. Whether they are irises, lilies or carnations, or perhaps some invented flower, the artists have lavished on these motifs the vivid reds, pinks, purples and yellows drawn from nature. Less lifelike are the lines of *buta* motifs resembling imaginary flowering plants that serve as borders of sashes and shawls produced in Kashmir. Woven in brilliantly coloured woollen threads on pale backgrounds, these *butas* represent a somewhat extreme floral stylization.

Rows of natural flowers with petals and leaves, on bright red backgrounds, are preferred for woven carpets. Though the flowers may have blossoms woven in white, yellow and blue threads, and invariably set against brilliant red backgrounds, the overall impression is somehow one of an actual garden with flowers planted in regular rows, arranged about a central axis. Among the most accomplished achievements of the Mughal *karkhanas*, these garden carpets attain a satisfactory visual balance between floral motifs drawn from nature and the demands of the woven medium, in which decorative elements need necessarily be regularly repeated. Carpets sometimes even serve as an inspiration for murals, such as the panels that adorn the interior of Akbar's tomb.

Among the most enchanting examples of floral decor in Mughal style are those at diminutive scale executed in watercolours in the painted borders of calligraphic pages and miniature paintings. Here artists evidently felt sufficiently free to create imaginary Gardens of Delight, with rows of different coloured flowers that only occasionally conform to those in nature. Sometimes the palette is restricted to a gold monochrome, applied in transparent watercolour on dark blue or green backgrounds, so as to achieve a magical, unearthly quality that nonetheless pays homage to the teeming world of reality. Even more luxurious are the floral designs fashioned out of precious gems. Though the technique here is constrained by the hard stone medium with which the artists had to work, the assemblages of gems in gold frames often attain a lyrical elegance that subtly suggests actual floral forms. This is best seen in the spectacular turban ornaments inset with rubies, diamonds and emeralds worn by the Mughal emperors and their nobles. Dagger hilts, *huqqa* bowls and even writing boxes of pale white or deep green jade are also the vehicles of floral schemes, enhanced by blossoms of tiny rubies or pieces of lapis lazuli, generally secured by tiny gold strips. Even when devoid of gems, jade could be sculpted into the semblance of lifelike, curling leaves or open flowers of considerable elegance, as in the bowls and wine cups, some specially fashioned for the emperors themselves, according to their engraved inscriptions. Floral motifs also embellish glass objects, especially *huqqa* bowls painted with gilt and covered with realistic depictions of lotuses or poppies, as well as more stylized grids of single blossoms and leaves.

Vessels enhanced with brilliantly coloured enamel inlays serve as an ideal vehicle for lustrous floral designs. A favourite scheme is that of red blossoms with green leaves on sparkling white or pure gold backgrounds. The flowers are arranged in regular formations repeated around the body of a tray or the sides of a box, or spread as radiating blossoms over the entire surface of a dish. In miniature form, the same enamelled motifs even embellish the rear faces of jewelled necklaces and head ornaments. This floral decor is sustained even when the colour scheme is restricted to silver and brass inlays, as in the dazzling *bidri* wares manufactured in the workshops of the Deccan. These are decorated with sprays of symmetrically arranged blossoms in repeated compartments on bowls, or distributed as blossoms that spread evenly across the circular interiors of dishes. The contrast between the gleaming inlays and the dark metallic background helps to distinguish the different patterns of petals and leaves. Here again, as in architecture and the other decorative arts, Mughal artists succeeded in inventing a floral milieu that delights and refreshes.

Like a great mantle draped over the monument is this magnificent floral panel created in white marble inlays on a red sandstone background on the principal gateway to Akbar's tomb at Sikandra. The central flower consists of six multi-lobed blossoms arranged in perfect formation around a central six-petalled flower; the surrounding leaves and stalks are more freely disposed. Though this does not represent a plant that is actually found in nature, the composition nonetheless evokes a paradisiacal world filled with flowers, an ideal introduction to the tomb of the emperor set within the great formal garden that lies beyond the gateway.

Fruits also have a role to play in Mughal floral decor, as in these red sandstone panels from the Turkish Sultana's house in Akbar's imperial residence at Fatehpur Sikri. These panels represent pomegranates (**left**) and grapes (**opposite**), both of which were probably cultivated in the palace gardens, and were no doubt enjoyed by the emperor and his courtiers, let alone the queen who is supposed to have inhabited this delightful pavilion. The botanical accuracy of these fruits demonstrates the skills of the Mughal craftsmen, who inherited the ancient Indian tradition of realistic stone carving in shallow relief.

While red sandstone was the preferred material of Akbar for his major architectural projects, it was also retained by Shah Jahan, as in these panels adorning the mosque adjacent to the Taj Mahal. The spray topped with an iris-like flower (**opposite**), has secondary blossoms of no particular species, disposed in a symmetrical, but nonetheless graceful manner. In the detail from another panel (**above**) the topmost flower seems to be a variation on a lily, executed in lifelike relief that captures the natural forms of the petals and leaves.

The white marble wall panels in the Taj Mahal are among the greatest masterpieces of floral art in Mughal style. Bunches of different flowers springing forth from ornamental vases are accorded the highest importance, being reserved for the interior of the upper tomb chamber. The central cluster in this panel is topped by an iris-hybrid form, but the accessory blooms are probably intended to represent lilies (*see also* Title page). The flowers in the two side vases, apparently tulips, are distributed symmetrically about the central stalk. Similar floral compositions, but without vases, are reserved for the exterior panels (*see* pp. 52—53).

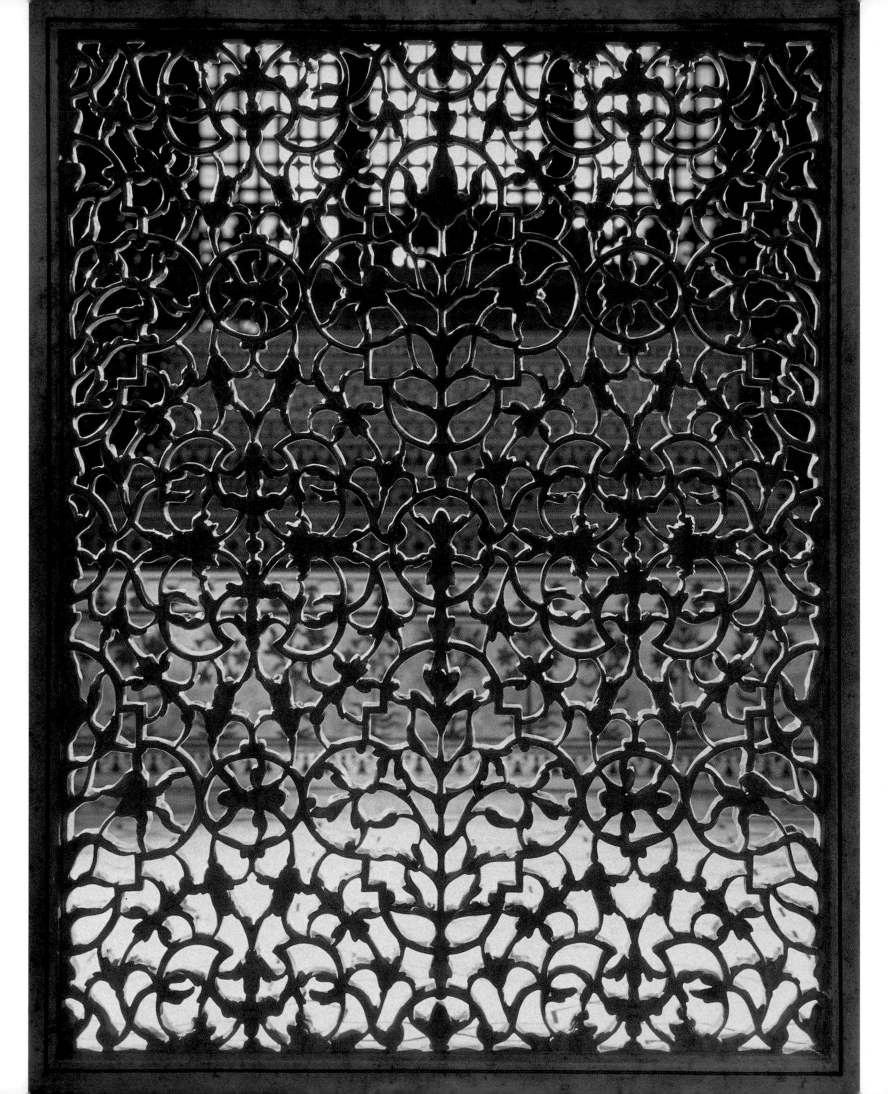

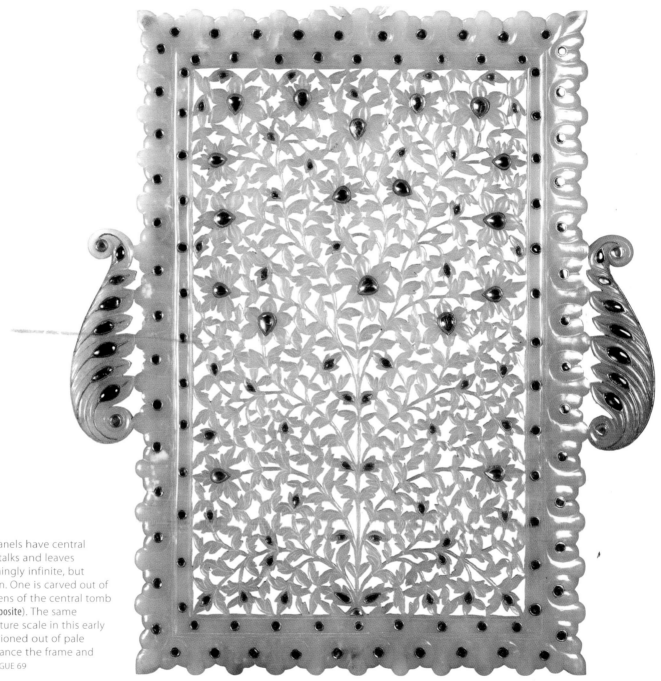

Both these intricate foliate panels have central vertical stems with stylized stalks and leaves emanating outwards in seemingly infinite, but strictly symmetrical formation. One is carved out of white marble on the *jali* screens of the central tomb chamber in the Taj Mahal (**opposite**). The same design also occurs at a miniature scale in this early 19th-century mirror-back fashioned out of pale green jade (**right**). Rubies enhance the frame and cut-out leafy handles. CATALOGUE 69

The parapet that runs along the top of the *jali* screens that encase the upper cenotaphs of Shah Jahan and Mumtaz Mahal in the Taj is conceived as a line of vase-shaped crenellations with trilobed tops. They are filled with flowers of different types executed in dazzling *pietra dura* technique, employing agate, carnelian, jasper and other semiprecious stones. The crenellations alternate with monochrome openwork, formed of elegant, cut-out leafy volutes that echo the perforated designs of the screens beneath.

FOLD OUT In spite of the hard stones out of which they are assembled, the flowers in the parapet elements of the screens portray with convincing naturalism the flowing petals and curling leaves of actual plants: from left to right, the lotus, crown imperial, narcissus and lily. The different colours of the minute pieces of semiprecious stones are manipulated with outstanding virtuosity to achieve a convincing botanical realism. This naturalism is matched in the frieze of poppies and lilies that adorns the sides of Shah Jahan's cenotaph itself (*see* Contents pages).

Many of the coloured stone inlays on the tomb of Itimad-ad Daula define wall panels with niche-like compartments headed by lobed arches (**left**). They accommodate fanciful blossoms, as well as sprays of flowers in vases, and even long-necked vases without flowers. The central niches are sometimes reserved for dark toned cypresses encircled by flowering bushes in paler colours (**below**). Since cemeteries in the Islamic world were often planted with cypresses, this was considered a particularly appropriate subject for a tomb.

Floral themes in tiled mosaic decorate Wazir Khan's mosque in Lahore. Here there is little attempt to imitate the natural world; rather, the tiles are exploited to achieve brilliant colouristic compositions, with purple blossoms on a yellow background, or white blossoms on a green background (**opposite**). Both plants have undulating stems and curling green leaves. A related topic is the spray of assorted flowers emerging from a cluster of green and turquoise leaves set in a fanciful vase (**right**). Here the different shaped blossoms are surrounded by curling blue clouds.

Flowers in vases are also a suitable motif for funerary monuments, as in these painted wall panels from the interior of Itimad-ad Daula's tomb. Here bright blue vases decorated with fish (**opposite**) and other fanciful motifs (**above**) contain bunches of flowers in gold and blue paint, the colours of which are now somewhat darkened. As in marble inlay and tile mosaic, floral realism is sacrificed for visual balance and symmetry; hence the orderly arrangement of blossoms, stalks and leaves. Even so, the flowers retain an unmistakable freshness that is almost naturalistic.

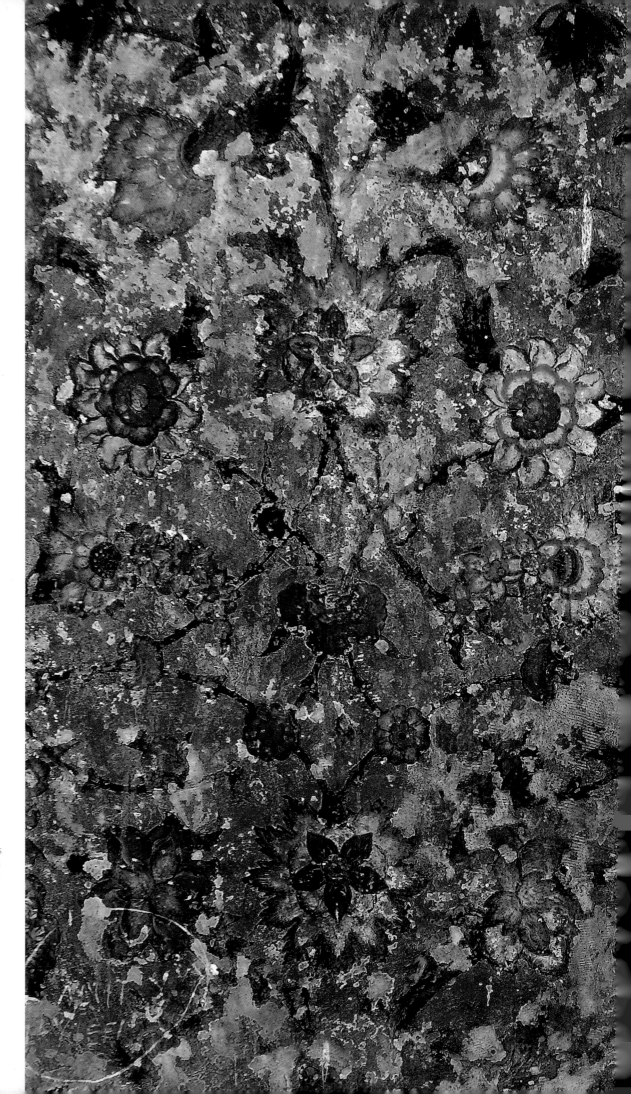

Another mural panel in Akbar's tomb presents a more conventional floral decor. This panel depicts imaginary blossoms with white, blue and red petals linked by swirling arcs of deep green stalks. The stalks are symmetrically disposed about the central blooms and terminate in stylized curling leaves. Though now somewhat faded, the gold tinted background still provides a brilliant setting for the composition, which recalls contemporary floral carpet design (*see, for example*, pp. 64—65).

Printed cotton hangings and floorspreads are often embellished with flowers-in-pot motifs, mostly in red on white backgrounds, as in these 17th- and 18th-century examples. In the hanging showing eight-petalled flowers set within an arched frame the blooms fan out in regular formation, the spaces in between being filled with leafy green stalks (**below**). The floorspread has fanciful and varied blooms, branching out freely, though symmetrically, over the white ground (**detail right**). This concern for balance even governs the subsidiary flowering plants and leafy stalks. CATALOGUE 25 & 26

Single flowering plants set in frames headed by lobed arches are found in embroidered wall hangings, whether in cotton (**opposite**) or silk (**left**). Dating from the 17th century, these textiles portray geometrically organized plants, either with red, hibiscus-like flowers on a white background, or with white multi-petalled blooms, partly resembling lotuses, on a red background, thereby maintaining the ubiquitous red and white colour combination of Mughal style. A similarly symmetrical composition is also found on a contemporary embossed brass panel on a door in the Bibi-ka Maqbara in Aurangabad (*see* p. 288). CATALOGUE 33 & 31

Silken threads enhancing 17th- and 18th-century velvets and brocades often contribute a lustrous sheen to floral themes. Lines of flowers in diagonal formation, each with identically arranged petals and leaves, run across this deep red velvet bolster (**below**). More naturalistically depicted are the irises and poppies with cream and luminous pink tones on a golden background of this brocaded hanging (**opposite**). Such velvet cushions and textiles once adorned the audience halls and pleasure pavilions of Mughal palaces, contributing towards the overall floral decor. CATALOGUE 40 & 32

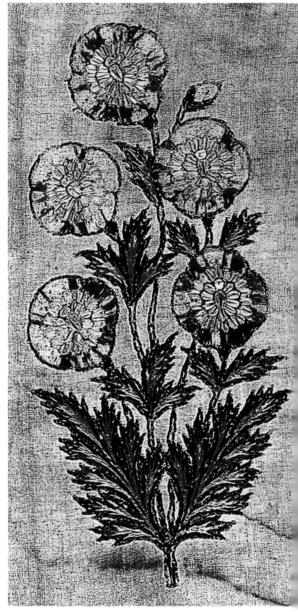

Rows of identical flowers of different types, depicted in a comparatively realistic manner, adorn the *patkas*, or waist-sashes, worn by the Mughal nobility. These borders of sashes dating from the 18th and 19th century show pairs of flowers, with curling sprays (**above left**), poppies (**centre**) and irises (**opposite**), printed in brilliant tones of blue, pink and purple onto plain backgrounds. Such decoration served as a perfect accompaniment to the floral motifs woven into the costumes and the floral themes of the turban ornaments and daggers worn by the emperor and his nobles. CATALOGUE 35, 36 & 29

Variant floral forms adorn the sashes and shawls
made in Kashmir during Mughal times. Here stylized
flowering plants known as *butas* filled with bunches
of blossoms are woven in brightly coloured woollen
threads on cream or pale blue backgrounds. While
the floral density of the *butas* on these three 18th-
century textiles does not accord with the natural
world, the overall effect evokes the visual pleasures
of an imagined garden. CATALOGUE 37, 39 & 38

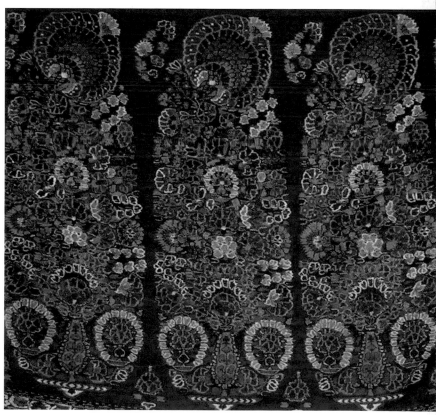

This garden carpet dating from the mid-17th century (**opposite**) presents plants of different types, some with tulip-like blossoms, others resembling pink poppies or purple irises. The flowers are aligned in rows on a deep red ground, the overall composition being repeated just over twice along the full length of the central panel. More stylized floral forms run along the border; here pale blossoms of no particular species are linked by swirling stalks with green and black leaves. Almost exactly the same stylized motifs form the principal subject of another, slightly earlier carpet (*see* pp. 64—65). CATALOGUE 20 & 24

When painted onto plaster, as on the vaults of the Badshahi mosque in Lahore, floral motifs are often reduced to conventional patterns. Here, a central medallion with an eight-petalled flower, contained by darkly-toned cartouches, is surrounded by irregularly shaped compartments filled with free-flowing leafy stems emanating from deep red flowers (**left**). Elsewhere in the mosque, these compartments are transformed into cartouches with alternating pointed and rounded sides (**below**). The same deep red tone is repeated for the flowers set on plain white backgrounds.

These monochrome, gold tinted flowers from the borders of an early 17th-century miniature and a similarly dated calligraphic page contrast effectively with the dark blue and dark green backgrounds. While the blossoms recall poppies and irises, the plants are essentially imaginary, in contrast to the realistic insects (**below**) and birds (**opposite**). Even so, a convincing naturalism is achieved by the elegantly swaying stalks and varied leafy forms, all created in gold paint ranging from opaque gouache to transparent watercolour. CATALOGUE 10 & 9

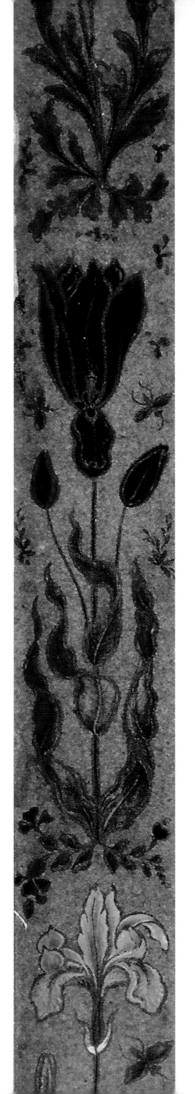

Borders from a 17th-century portrait of the emperor Shah Jahan and a page of calligraphy show diverse flowers on pale backgrounds where colour is used to distinguish the different flora, such as the bright red crocus and poppy (left). and the pink rose and narcissus (opposite), While the regular repetition of flowers in long rows robs these compositions of any convincing naturalism, there is the overall idea of a paradisiacal garden appropriate for both representations of royal figures and lines of Persian poetry. CATALOGUE 5 & 8

Imaginative floral patterns also serve as borders, as in this example from a calligraphic page painted in a Deccan workshop at the beginning of the 18th century. Here, bright red and blue blossoms, outlined in white and curling in different directions, are linked by trailing leafy stems, all set on a vibrant warm background. Avoiding any suggestion of botanical accuracy, the artist is here concerned to create an overall, dazzling colouristic effect, not unlike that of a textile or carpet. CATALOGUE 4

Precious gems are sometimes cut and assembled into elegantly designed foliate ornaments. This 18th-century turban jewel has a central ruby engraved with a full flower displaying ten regular petals (**right**). From this emerges a gold frame fashioned as a curving floral spray set with smaller rubies and diamonds, terminating in a pendant pearl. The leaves beneath are cut out of emeralds, while the pin itself, which is of jade, is also inset with rubies. A spectacular emerald that reached the Mughal court from the New World was intended as the centrepiece for a necklace. It was delicately engraved at some time in the late 16th century with a grove of palm-like trees (**detail opposite**). CATALOGUE 49 & 47

This upper arm ornament with enamelled side
handles for a strap, dating from the early 17th
century, is expertly carved in three dimensions out of
milky jade in the semblance of an open flower. While
the rings of petals interlock in a lifelike manner, the
central ruby ensures that this is no portrait of an
actual flower. Even so, an overall naturalistic
character is attained through the seemingly
effortless technique of cutting the flawless jade.
CATALOGUE 67

Rubies, diamonds and semiprecious stones contained in gold strips create a floral spray that emerges from a line of blossoms in the middle of the lid of this white jade pen box (above). Conforming to a perfectly symmetrical pattern, the blossoms and leaves are linked by minute strips of gold that serve as curling stalks. Similar floral motifs created from tiny rubies decorate the jade-handled knife, pen and burnisher, and the jade topped ink and sand pots inside the pen box (below). CATALOGUE 70

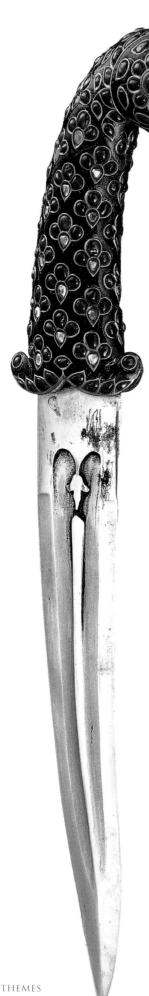

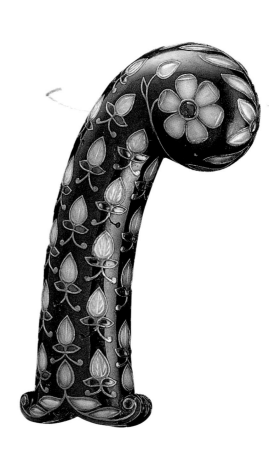

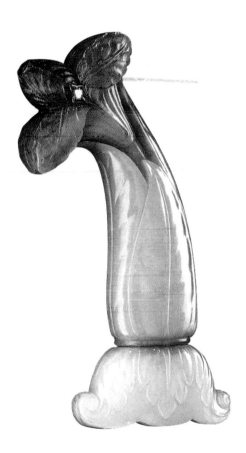

Dagger hilts dating from the 17th and early 18th century are vehicles for floral ornament created from precious stones set into gold strips, or sculpted out of jade. Rubies and pieces of white jade cut into the semblance of minute blossoms and leaves, with larger blossoms reserved for the bulbous pommels, decorate the hilts of three of these daggers (**opposite**). In two other examples the pommels are carved in shallow relief as a triple-petalled flower emerging from a petalled base, or a curling stem terminating in a five-petalled bloom (**left**). CATALOGUE 94, 54, 55, 56, & 57

Glass *huqqa* bowls dating from the 18th century also serve as settings for luxurious floral ornament, especially when gilded. One example in clear glass is adorned with naturalistic red and gold lotuses with tall stalks and green leaves that appear to float in an actual lotus pond (**detail opposite**). Another example in blue glass has a pattern of gilded, four-petalled blossoms spread evenly over the body of the bowl (**left**). *Huqqa* bowls of green glass are also popular since the dark background serves as an effective contrast to the gilt floral motifs (*see* pp. 62—63). They are either painted as realistic poppies onto the glass itself, or cut out from the gilded coating to reveal a grid of pointed leaves. CATALOGUE 45 & 46

Regular arrangements of bright red blossoms and deep green leaves adorn this octagonal tray (**above**) and circular dish (**detail opposite**), both assigned to the 17th century. Here the colours are applied in enamels onto pure gold and shining white backgrounds, so as to achieve brilliant contrasts. Repeated sprays of flowers are arranged in the outer compartments of the tray, or, as isolated blossoms, spread in radial fashion across the central field of the dish. A more fluid composition of blossoms and curling leafy stalks fills the circular surface of another gold dish (*see* pp. 58—59). CATALOGUE 87, 88 & 89

Enamelled designs with red flowers on bright white backgrounds, relieved by occasional deep green leaves, adorn the rear faces of this 18th-century gold necklace (**above**). Here the floral elements are densely packed so as to entirely fill the curving areas of the side pieces and pendants, all of which are fringed by tiny pearls. The same bright red enamels are also used to portray the repeating sprays of regularly arranged flowers that fill the tray, side compartments and lid of this 17th-century octagonal *pandan* (**detail opposite**). CATALOGUE 52 & 90

Jewelry formed out of gold frames containing precious stones as well as tiny enamel pieces often take foliate forms. The back of this *sarpech*, or turban ornament, has enamelled elements in brilliant red, white and green colours portraying a line of three floral motifs, the interiors of which are inhabited by tiny birds (**opposite**). The curving floral spray at the top terminates in a pendant carved emerald, whlle unshaped spinels line the underside of the ornament. Also intended for adorning a turban is this floral pin, with a symmetrically disposed spray of eight-petalled flowers fashioned out of diamonds and rubies (**right**). CATALOGUE 51 & 50

Metallic weapons are often adorned with floral designs realized in gold hammered into steel, according to the technique known as damascening. The hilts of these two swords dating from the 17th century are enhanced by gleaming floral motifs on dark backgrounds. They each show two full blossoms, surrounded by smaller blooms on curving stalks (**right**), or leafy extensions (**opposite**). Such motifs entirely cover both front and back of each hilt.
CATALOGUE 96 & 97

The finest *bidri* vessels dating from the 17th and 18th centuries present floral designs realized in lustrous silver and brass inlays. This *huqqa* bowl has oval cartouches, regularly repeated around the circular body, filled with plants composed of triple blossoms (**above**). The circular powder box with lobed sides presents orderly compartments, in which lotus-like flowers with long stalks alternate with multi-petalled blossoms interspersed with leafy stems (**detail opposite**). CATALOGUE 81 & 80

FOLLOWING PAGES In this *bidri* dish assigned to the 17th century, tiny six-petalled silver flowers with pairs of brass leaves extend all the way across the circular surface to generate a floral pattern of uniform visual density. A medallion with multiple rings of petals occupies the centre of the dish, while a line of blossoms linked by leafy stalks runs continuously around the rim. The luminous inlays on the dark metallic background highlight the individual floral elements. CATALOGUE 82

Animals & Birds

Though perfectly aware of the prohibition on the representation of human figures, animals and birds that was dictated by Islamic orthodoxy, the Mughals were especially receptive to illustrations of the natural world; indeed, the emperors and their courtiers took a particular delight in animal and bird forms. In this regard they followed the practice of their Central Asian ancestors, who had in earlier times commissioned sumptuous art objects decorated with animal motifs. But the Mughals also inherited the long-standing fascination with nature in all of its manifestations that characterizes ancient Indian mythology, literature and art. In the expert hands of carvers, painters and weavers employed in the imperial *karkhanas*, most of them Indians, the repertory of animals and birds familiar from Central Asian and Persian art was extended to include indigenous fauna, such as the lion, panther, elephant and water buffalo, as well as the peacock, parrot and mynah. Here, too, mythical beasts with a long history in Indian art, like the *vyala*, with a leonine body and ferocious head, took their place beside fantastic creatures of Persian and ultimate Chinese origin, such as the flying *simurgh* with its grotesque beak, extended feathery wings and trailing tail that became a particular feature of Mughal art. Woven in coloured silk and woollen threads, painted in subtle watercolours or chiselled out of jade or ivory, these diverse fauna, both natural and imagined, were imbued with the unmistakable vitality and realism that are the distinctive hallmarks of Mughal style.

Jahangir is well known for his interest in nature and the studies of particular species of animals and birds that he commissioned. These occupy a unique place in the history of Mughal pictorial art, whether they be 'portraits' of a falcon (*see* p. 15), a peacock with peahen, or a *nilgai* deer. Admittedly, animal themes were already familiar in the fine arts and architectural decor of Akbar's era, as may be found in the sculpted sandstone elephant and peacock brackets in the apartments of this emperor at Agra and Lahore, and in the painted landscape scenes crowded with assorted fauna that illustrate animal fables such as the

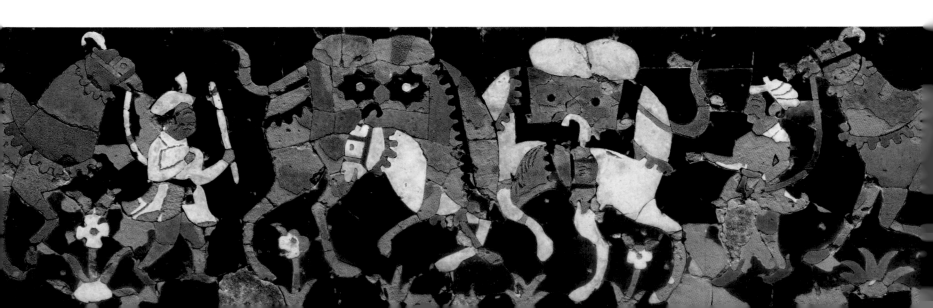

Anwar-i Suhayli or Akbar's biographical *Akbar Nama*. Animals and birds also occupy the painted borders that frame Persian calligraphic compositions, and even portraits of the emperors themselves and his nobles; they sometimes intrude into the text itself, being painted between the scrolls and tails of *nasta`liq* styled letters, no doubt to the delight of the viewer. That particular animals such as the lion or leaping tiger could augment the image of the emperor himself is demonstrated in the coins of the period, especially the gold *mohurs* issued by Jahangir on which these and other animals emblematic of the imperial presence make an appearance. From time to time such animals are chosen to adorn particular objects intended for personal royal use. The personal wine cup of Shah Jahan crafted from pure white jade, for example, is conceived as an open lotus, its petalled sides converging on a naturalistic ram's head with cut-out curving horns (*see* p. 216).

Animal compositions combining wild beasts contained in circles arranged in rows, separated by pairs of formally disposed birds, form the subject of silken cloths woven in the Mughal *karkhanas* and in textile centres like Banaras and Ahmedabad. This theme, originating in the ancient art of the Near East, was transmitted to Mughal India via Persia where it enjoyed considerable popularity. More characteristic of Mughal style are the great garden carpets with fruit trees and flowering bushes populated by animals and birds. Such compositions derive from the Garden of Delight compositions that were ubiquitous in Persian art, and which were eagerly imitated by Mughal artists and craftsmen. Nowhere is this better seen than in the magnificent carpets woven in the imperial *karkhanas* in Agra and Lahore, offering paradisiacal visions of an idealized natural world. Such carpets were intended for the emperor and his nobles and sons to sit on, perhaps accompanied by the ruler's favourite wives or concubines. With their central panels portraying brightly coloured, miscellaneous flora and fauna, these woven gardens served as tranquil settings for conversation, refreshments and other pleasures.

Animal fights are a popular theme in Mughal style, especially when depicted on the walls of royal palaces, near which such combats actually took place for the amusement of the emperor and his nobles. These panels in coloured tile mosaic from Lahore Fort show double-humped, Central Asian camels, two of which have their heads interlocked in conflict (**opposite**), and a pair of elephants directed into combat by diminutive riders (**below**).

One particular carpet has a central panel showing generously spreading trees with pale blossoms and flowering plants on a brilliant red background. This landscape is inhabited by large showy birds in the middle — notably, a pair of cranes, a peacock and peahen, and a cock and hen in the middle — and smaller birds of various types at the bottom and top. While there is no attempt here to represent an actual natural setting, every effort is made to achieve evenly spaced motifs that are appropriate to the woven medium. The same is true of a much longer pictorial carpet, also with flowering trees and plants, and even palm trees, on a sombre, wine red background. Birds sit on the branches of the trees, while beneath antelopes scurry away from tigers, one of which is shown savagely attacking its prey. Into this realistic fauna scurries the odd mythical beast, such as a winged, leonine *vyala*. Here the visual structure of the woven composition is clearly evident, with the same combination of trees, birds and animals being repeated more than three times along the full length of the carpet.

Scenery in itself had a role to play in Mughal style as is demonstrated in the sandstone wall panels in Akbar's palace at Fatehpur Sikri, some of which are carved as fantastic landscapes, the ideal habitat for animals and birds, even if these do not always make an appearance (*see* pp. 50–51). Comparable compositions with trees and flowering bushes executed in delicate transparent monochrome fill the borders of calligraphic pages and manuscript illustrations. These scenes are sometimes inhabited by lions and tigers, deer and antelope; comparable skyscapes are crowded with birds of different species, including the *simurghs* that have already been noticed. Humans occasionally intrude as hunters accompanied by dogs, or as labourers carrying out seasonal tasks, rather in the manner of the European engravings that found their way to the Mughal court. In spite of these human elements, the principal theme in such compositions remains the natural world.

Landscapes populated by a variety of fauna are also realized in other materials and techniques. A riding coat, richly embroidered all over with fine silk chain-stitching in elegant pale pink, orange and green tones, portrays flowering plants and trees with blossoms, the spaces in between being crammed with fleeing antelope, flying birds and even the odd animal fight. The result is a visual density that is both sumptuous and soothing. Virtually the same scene with equally varied animals and birds is created in gleaming coloured enamel inlays set into a silver *huqqa* bowl. In both the riding coat and *huqqa* bowl there is a total absence of human figures; the flora and fauna evidently provide sufficient visual interest. Miniature objects with more brightly coloured enamelled inlays, especially brilliant reds and greens on white, and even rubies and emeralds set into gold frames, also portray the natural world. Particularly popular are the compositions with hawks, parrots and other birds surrounded by blossoms and swirling leaves so as to suggest actual plants and trees. Such objects include exquisitely worked, tiny jewelled lockets and boxes.

More remarkable from an artistic point of view are the animal 'portraits' sculpted out of different coloured jades to serve as the hilts of daggers and swords with steel blades. Whether it is the head of a horse, ram or *nilgai*, these three-dimensional, miniature animal studies are infused with a compelling naturalism that sets Mughal style apart from its Central Asian and Persian antecedents. Such animal-handled weapons were hardly suitable as instruments of war; their purpose appears to have been essentially ceremonial, being worn by the emperor and his nobles at all formal occasions as signs of personal status and wealth. Assemblages of more stylized animals and birds are carved onto the sides of the ivory primers that were taken on hunting expeditions for the storing of gunpowder used in rifles. Here are found miniature relief scenes of actual expeditions, with hunters clutching their spoils, or dogs running after deer and other wild animals; tigers also make an appearance, falling hungrily on their prey. The tapering ends of these primers are carved in almost three dimensions with snakes, monkeys, water birds and antelope heads. All of these animal and bird themes are ingeniously fitted into the curving profiles of the elephant tusks out of which the primers are fashioned.

Scenes of hunting occupy a privileged place in the pictorial compositions that constitute yet another dimension of Mughal style. Not only were hunting outings a popular recreation for the emperor and his nobles, they also served as essential training ground for young princes, who could on these occasions be schooled in riding and in the expert handling of bows and arrows or guns. Perhaps for this reason hunters make an appearance in the scenes that adorn a series of wooden boxes that were apparently much prized at the Mughal court. In a cabinet with painted and lacquered sides, for example, young men wearing typical Mughal tunics and turbans, and armed with bows and arrows, are shown mounted on horses riding through a forest of flowering plants, through which deer and rabbits flee in alarm. Two of the horsemen are attacked by lions in particularly ruthless depictions of combat. Less vigorous are the scenes on another box with drawers, the fronts of which have figures assembled from minute ivory pieces showing hunters with guns and bows and arrows running after leaping tigers and *nilgai*. Such excursions must also have included pleasurable interludes since one inlaid scene depicts a nobleman with a female companion, peacefully conversing on a raised seat in a garden setting, surrounded by flowering trees, seemingly undisturbed by the activity all around them.

These painted and inlaid hunting compositions may be compared with the scene engraved onto the circular body of a copper wine bowl. Here hunters mounted on horses or riding elephants, bearing spears and bows and arrows, chase deer through a countryside entirely filled with trees, bushes, fantasy flowers and flying birds. Though superficially resembling the garden compositions found in textiles, carpets and metallic vessels, the landscape here focuses more on the venture of the chase than on harmony and delight.

Pairs of fighting animals, or animals pursuing one another, form the principal topics of the border from this mid-17th-century textile from Chanderi, a provincial city known for its fine cottons woven with gold threads. The animals contained in circles include pairs of wild buffaloes, bears and antelopes, as well as a tiger pursuing a deer, and a lion eating a tiger. The animals are contained in regularly spaced circles separated by pairs of formally disposed birds, following an ancient Persian composition. The predominant red colour scheme, however, is typical of Mughal style. CATALOGUE 27

Landscapes inhabited by animals and birds make a
regular appearance in Mughal miniature painting, as
in these pages from two *Anwar-i Suhayli* manuscripts
dating from the end of the 16th century. One
illustrates the congregation of birds that attended
the return of eggs to a partridge, which had lost
them to the ocean (**above**). The composition displays
the artist's ability to accurately portray the different
cranes, pelicans, peacocks, owl, hoopoe and other
birds. Equally realistic is Miskin's depiction of the
court of the lions, complete with tigers, deer,
monkey and cow, all gathered peacefully in a rocky
setting (**opposite**). CATALOGUE 12 & 13

This carpet dating from the early 17th century has a central panel showing a landscape populated by a pair of cranes, a peacock and peahen, and a cock and hen. The birds are arranged around a tree with spreading branches and pale green blossoms (**left & detail opposite**). Additional smaller birds crowd the flowering trees and bushes at the top and bottom. This serene prospect presents an image of a Garden of Delight, the perfect accompaniment to the pleasures enjoyed by the Mughal emperor and his courtiers who would have sat on exactly such a carpet, perhaps in an actual garden setting.
CATALOGUE 21

This detail from a mid-17th century illuminated page shows a crowd of birds winging their way across a landscape filled with plants and flowers. Fantastic *simurghs*, recognized by their grotesque beaks, feathery wings and trailing tails, dominate real birds, including ducks and water fowl. Because the artist has rendered all these aerial creatures in transparent gold brushstrokes, the scene has an almost transcendental quality. This complements the delicately rendered *shamsa* surrounded by arabesque ornament that occupies the middle of the page (*see* p. 22). CATALOGUE 1

Animals, birds and even winged insects in a whimsical natural setting filled with flowering plants and bushes are realized in fine, pale silk embroidery in this early 17th-century riding coat, woven for a Mughal prince during Jahangir's reign (**opposite**). These fauna also serve as the principal topics of the gleaming enamel inlays set into a silver *huqqa* bowl made in a Lucknow workshop during the late 18th century (**right**). In spite of differences in material and technique, the riding coat and *huqqa* bowl present virtually the same vision of an imaginary landscape teeming with flowers, plants and wildlife of various kinds. CATALOGUE 34 & 92

Enamelled lockets and medallions (**below & opposite top**) and miniature boxes (**opposite bottom**) are often adorned with parrots in floral settings. The swirling sprays of leaves and blossoms echo the curving profiles of the birds themselves, shown here in a lifelike manner with their heads raised up or pointed down. Even so, the vivid red and green enamels on brilliant white backgrounds give these miniature 18th-century objects a brightly patterned, decorative quality. This is also true of the jewelled fronts of lockets, such as the example showing a falcon fashioned out of rubies in a gold frame (**above**).
CATALOGUE 48, 53 & 91

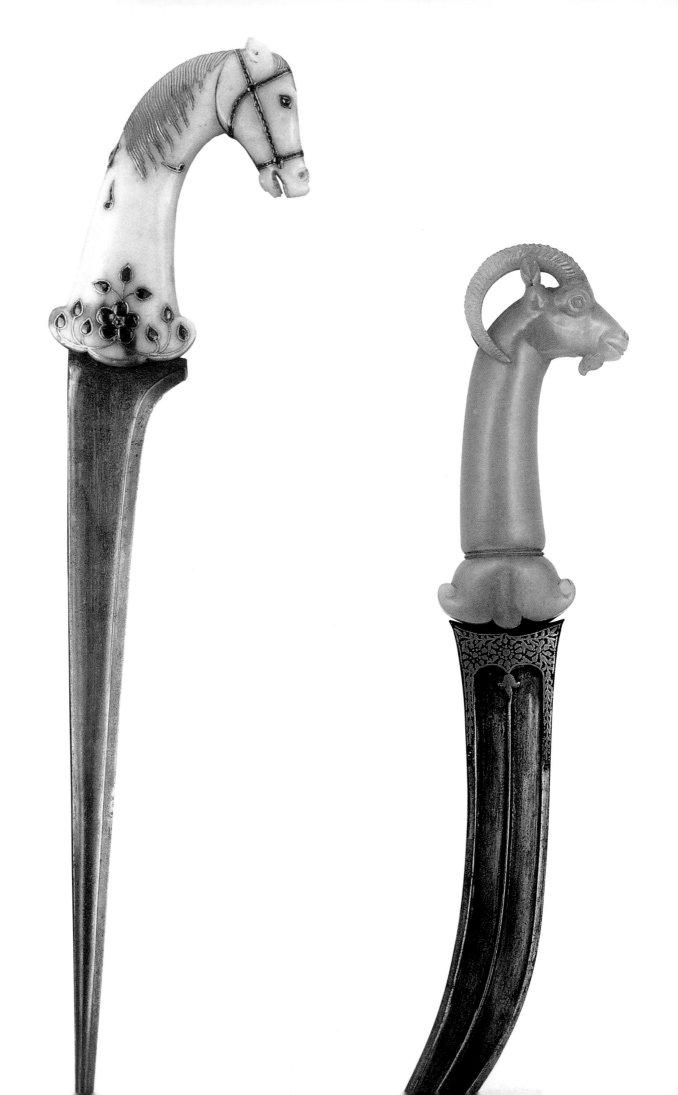

Animal heads adorning the pommels of these jade dagger hilts are carved in a convincing lifelike manner, confirming the naturalism that is an essential attribute of Mughal style. Whether depicting horses, rams or *nilgai*, these miniature animal 'portraits' are perfectly rendered in three dimensions, the mouths, eyes, ears and manes all truthfully depicted, sometimes even picked out with rubies and gold strips. The animals, which all face towards the steel blades of the daggers, were mostly sculpted in the 17th century. CATALOGUE 58, 59, 60 & 61

Curving ivory horns sometimes serve as vehicles for relief animal and bird carvings, as in these two mid-17th-century primers used for storing gunpowder. That such objects were used in hunting is evident in the actual subjects carved in shallow relief on their curved sides, such as tigers pursuing deer, or hunters carrying their spoils. Monkeys and the heads of rams and antelopes are skilfully worked into the sides of the horns, either juxtaposed in tightly compressed compositions, or cut out in almost three dimensions to fit the tapering ends of the horns themselves.
CATALOGUE 72 & 73

Hunting scenes with animals adorn the lids of wooden
cabinets that were much prized at the Mughal court.
In the early 17th-century example with a painted and
lacquered lid (**above**) huntsmen bearing bows and
arrows ride horses that leap through a forested
landscape. On the front of the cabinet with minute ivory
inlays also dating from the early 17th century (**opposite**),
running huntsmen are shown aiming rifles at fleeing
tigers and deer. In the central top panel, a couple is
shown seated in conversation within a flowering grove.
CATALOGUE 16 & 17

FOLLOWING PAGES The continuous, engraved scene
running around the curving body of this copper
bowl is also devoted to hunting. Here riders on
horses and elephants proceed through a landscape
entirely filled with flowers and flying birds, through
which *nilgai* flee. The *nasta`liq* inscription on the
upper rim quotes Persian verses in praise of the wine
that was undoubtedly intended to be drunk from the
vessel. Other verses indicate the religious learning of
the owner of the vessel, and 1582 as the date of its
manufacture. CATALOGUE 77

DOCUMENTATION

CATALOGUE OF OBJECTS

**ILLUMINATION &
CALLIGRAPHY**

1 Shah Jahan album
Shamsa (rosette) with *tughra* (calligraphic signature)
Ink, gouache, and gold on paper
39.1 cm high, 26.7 cm wide
Northern India, mid-17th century
New York, The Metropolitan Museum of Art (Purchase, Rogers Fund and The Kevorkian Foundation Gift, 1955), 15.121.10.39
PAGES 22, 153, 248—249

2 Page from Munajat-i-Hazrat Ali
Ink and gouache on paper
22.2 cm high, 14.7 cm wide
Northern India, 16th century
Hyderabad, Salar Jung Museum, 896B/XLIX (LIX/896)
PAGE 154

3 Specimen of calligraphy
Ascribed to Mir Ali
Ink and gouache on paper
26 cm high, 16 cm wide
Northern India, dated 1536
New Delhi, National Museum, 56.62/58
PAGE 157

MINIATURE PAINTING

7 Shah Jahan on the Peacock Throne
From the *Padshahnama*, Vol. II
Attributed to 'Abid, son of Aqa Raza
Opaque watercolour and gold on paper
36.7 cm high, 25 cm wide
Northern India, 1639-40
California, San Diego Museum of Art (Edwin Binney 3rd Collection), 1990:352
PAGE 10

8 Portrait of Shah Jahan
Artist: Bichitir
Gouache and watercolour on paper
22 cm high, 13 cm wide
Northern India, ca. 1631
London, Victoria and Albert Museum, IM.17-1925
PAGE 208

9 Portrait of Mirza Ghazi
Artist: Manohar
Tempera, gold on blue borders
13.5 cm high, 6.4 cm wide
Northern India, ca. 1610-12
London, Victoria and Albert Museum, IM.118.1921
PAGE 207

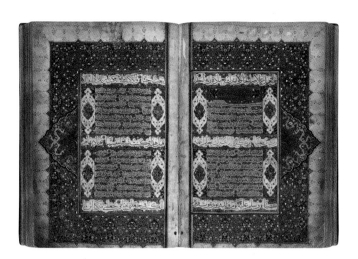

4 Specimen of calligraphy
Ink and watercolour on paper
44.2 cm high, 28.1 cm wide
Hyderabad, early 18ᵗʰ century
Mumbai, Chhatrapati Shivaji Maharaj Vastu
Sangrahalaya (Sir Ratan Tata Collection),
22.3395
PAGES 155, 210—211

5 Reverse of portrait of Zulfiqar Khan
Ink and watercolour on paper
22.4 cm high, 17.5 cm wide
Northern India, *ca.* 1615
London, Victoria and Albert Museum,
IM.2401925
PAGES 156, 209

6 Double page of a Koran
Ink, gouache, and gold on paper
33 cm high, 22 cm wide
Lahore, dated 1573-74
London, British Library, Add. 18497
ff 118v-119
PAGES 108—109, 138—139

10 A youth fallen from a tree
Shah Jahan album. Artist: Aqa Reza
Ink, colours, and gold on paper
39 cm high, 25.6 cm wide
Northern India, *ca.* 1610
New York, The Metropolitan Museum
of Art (Purchase, Rogers Fund and
The Kevorkian Foundation Gift, 1955),
15.121.10.20
PAGE 206

11 Peregrine falcon on perch
Artist: Mansur
Gouache on paper
35.5 cm high, 25.2 cm wide
Northern India, early 17ᵗʰ century
Mumbai, Chhatrapati Shivaji Maharaj Vastu
Sangrahalaya, 15.302
PAGE 15

12 Congregation of birds
From an illustrated manuscript of
Anwar-i-Suhayli
Gouache on paper
24.8 cm high, 15.7 cm wide
Northern India, *ca* 1575
Mumbai, Chhatrapati Shivaji Maharaj Vastu
Sangrahalaya (Gift from the collection of
Dr. Alma Latifi), 73.5/204
PAGE 242

13 Lion's court
Artist: Miskin
From an illustrated manuscript of the
Anwar-i Suhayli
Gouache on paper
29.4 cm high, 15.6 cm wide
Lahore, dated 1597
Varanasi, Bharat Kala Bhavan, 9069.9
PAGE 243

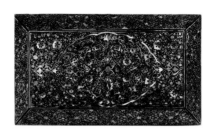

FURNITURE

14 Writing chest (qalamdan) with calligraphic decoration
Wood with mother-of-pearl inlays
36.5 cm high, 65.5 cm long, 36 cm wide
Gujarat, dated 1587
Athens, Benaki Museum, 10181
PAGES 158—159

15 Casket with arabesque design
Wood with mother-of-pearl inlays
35 cm high, 51 cm long, 29 cm wide
Gujarat, ca. 1600
London, Victoria and Albert Museum, 155-1866
PAGES 44—45

16 Cabinet with hunting scene
Painting on lacquered wood
20 cm high, 28.5 cm long, 21.5 cm wide
Deccan or Sindh, early 17th century
Oxford, Ashmolean Museum, EA 1978.129
PAGE 258

CARPETS

18 Carpet with floral motifs
Cotton (warp and weft), wool (pile)
447 cm long, 256.6 cm wide
Lahore (?), ca. 1640-45
Cincinnati Art Museum (Gift of Mrs Audrey Emery), 1952.201
PAGES 201—203

19 Floral (millefleur) carpet
Silk (warp and weft), *pashmina* wool (pile)
211 cm long, 147 cm wide
Lahore, Agra or Kashmir, late 17th century
Oxford, Ashmolean Museum, EA1975.17
PAGE 27

20 Carpet with flower pattern
Cotton (warp and weft), wool (pile)
436.9 cm long, 205.7 cm wide
Kashmir or Lahore, second half of 17th century
New York, The Metropolitan Museum of Art (Florance Waterbury Bequest and Rogers Fund, 1970), 1970.321
PAGE 200

17 Cabinet with hunting scene
Wood, ivory and brass
33.7 cm high, 46.7 cm long,
31.8 cm wide
Sindh (?), early 17th century
Cincinnati Art Museum (The William T. and
Louise Taft Semple Collection), 1962.457
PAGE 259

21 Carpet with landscape and birds
Cotton (warp and weft), wool (pile)
233 cm long, 158 cm wide
Northern India (Lahore), ca.1600
Vienna, MAK-Museum of Applied Arts,
Vienna, Or 292
PAGES 244, 247

22 Carpet with lattice design (fragment)
Silk (warp and weft), *pashmina* wool (pile)
302.3 cm long, 121.9 cm wide
Northern India, 17th century
New York, The Metropolitan Museum of
Art (Bequest of Benjamin Aitman, 1913,
and The Friedsam Collection, Bequest
of Michael Friedsam 1931), 14.40.712,
32.100.457
PAGE 104

23 Carpet with animals and trees
Cotton (warp and weft), wool (pile)
833.1 cm long, 289.5 cm wide
Lahore, 17th century
New York, The Metropolitan Museum
of Art (Gift of J. Pierpont Morgan, 1917),
17.190.858
PAGES 245, 246

**24 Carpet with scrolling vines
and blossoms**
Wool
922 cm long, 340.4 cm wide
Northern India, ca. 1620-30
New York, The Metropolitan Museum
of Art (Gift of J. Pierpont Morgan, 1917),
17.190.857
PAGES 64—65

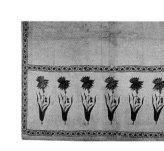

TEXTILES

25 Kanat (tent hanging) with flower motifs
Cotton, stencilled, and hand block-printed
108 cm high, 211 cm wide
Burhanpur, early 18th century
Mumbai, Chhatrapati Shivaji Maharaj Vastu
Sangrahalaya, 72.5
PAGE 190

26 Floorspread
Cotton cloth with painted resist and
mordants
690.9 cm long, 462.3 cm wide
Golconda, ca. 1630
Cincinnati Art Museum (The William T. and
Louise Taft Semple Collection), 1962.486
PAGES 124—125, 191

27 Textile with animal motifs
Cotton base, woven with golden threads
356 cm long, 54 cm wide
Chanderi, Madhya Pradesh, ca. 1650
New Delhi, National Museum, 51.229/D
PAGES 240—241

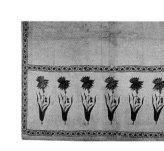

28 Shawl with chevron design
Pashm (wool)
146.2 cm long, 15.2 cm wide
Kashmir, 18th century
New Delhi, National Museum, 57.110/9
PAGE 68—69

29 Patka with border
Cotton, block-printed, mordant- and resist-
dyed, painted silk fringe ends
208.3 cm long, 64.4 cm wide
Rajasthan, 19th century
Ahmedabad, Calico Museum of Textiles, 504
PAGE 197 (RIGHT)

30 Patka with floral border
Cotton, partly stencilled and partly block-
printed, painted, mordant- and resist-dyed
264.3 cm long, 65.3 cm wide
Burhanpur, 18th century,
Ahmedabad, Calico Museum of Textiles, 694
PAGE 163

35 Patka with floral border
Cotton, block-printed, painted, mordant-
dyed
248 cm long, 61 cm wide
Burhanpur, 18th/19th century
Ahmedabad, Calico Museum of Textiles, 273
PAGE 196

36 Patka with floral border
Cotton, embroidered with silk and silver-
gilt thread
259.2 cm long, 57.3 cm wide
Rajasthan or Gujarat, 18th/19th century
Ahmedabad, Calico Museum of Textiles, 503
PAGES 196—197

37 Patka with floral border
Wool
644 cm long, 68 cm wide
Kashmir, 18th century
Mumbai, Chhatrapati Shivaji Maharaj Vastu
Sangrahalaya, 56.17
PAGE 198

31 Wall hanging with flowering plants
Silk, lampa silk loom finish
213.3 cm long, 91.4 cm wide
Agra or Lahore, 17th century
Varanasi, Bharat Kala Bhavan, 10/33
PAGE 193

32 Darbar hanging with iris flowers
Cotton, quilted and embroidered with silk
and silver-gilt thread
188.1 cm long, 120.7 cm wide
Gujarat, *ca.* 1628-58
Ahmedabad, Calico Museum of Textiles, 289
PAGE 195

33 Wall hanging with flowering plant
Cotton embroidered with silk
117 cm high, 81 cm wide
Northern India, second half of
17th century
London, Victoria and Albert Museum,
IS 168-1950
PAGE 192

34 Riding coat with animal and bird motifs
Satin embroidered with coloured silks
97 cm high
Northern India, early 17th century
London, Victoria and Albert Museum,
IS.18-1947
PAGE 250

38 Patka with floral border
Woollen, loom-woven
792.4 cm long, 73.6 cm wide
Kashmir, 18th century
Varanasi, Bharat Kala Bhavan, 10/641
PAGE 199 (BOTTOM)

39 Shawl with floral border
Woollen, loom-woven
331.4 cm long, 125.1 cm wide
Kashmir, 18th century
Varanasi, Bharat Kala Bhavan, 10/642
PAGE 199 (TOP)

40 Bolster with floral motifs
Velvet embroidered with gold and silk
109.3 cm long
Northern India, late 18th century
New Delhi, National Museum,
57.110/12
PAGE 194

CERAMIC & GLASS

41 Tile with flower
Earthenware and enamelled
9.6 cm high, 9.1 cm wide
Lahore, mid-17th century
London, Victoria and Albert Museum,
IS.57-1898
PAGE 56

42 Tile with floral design
Earthenware and enamelled
7.8 cm high, 7.6 cm wide
Lahore, mid-17th century
London, Victoria and Albert Museum,
IM.271-1923
PAGE 57

43 Huqqa base with leaf motifs
Green glass with gilt floral decoration
18.9 cm high, 17.8 cm diameter
Northern India, 18th century
London, Victoria and Albert Museum,
IM.15-1930
PAGE 62

GEMS & JEWELRY

47 Centrepiece element
Carved from emerald, drilled
5 cm high, 5.7 cm wide, 1 cm thick,
233.5 carats
Northern India, 8th-9th decade 16th century
Art Market, 1982
Kuwait, The al-Sabah Collection,
Dar al-Athar al-Islamiyyah, LNS 28 HS
PAGE 213

48 Pendant with flowers and bird
Gold with coloured enamels
3.7 cm high, 3 cm wide
Northern India, 17th century
London, British Museum, OA 14178
PAGE 252

**49 Jewel turban
ornament (kalgi)**
Gold set with rubies and
emeralds 20 cm high
Northern India, 18th century
London, Victoria and Albert
Museum, IS 02569
PAGE 212

44 Huqqa bowl with poppy plants
Green glass with gilt floral decoration
19 cm high, 18 cm diameter
Northern India, late 17th century
London, British Museum, OA 1961.10-16.1
PAGE 63

45 Huqqa base with lotus flowers
Clear glass with polychrome enamel and
gilding
20.32 cm high 17.15 cm wide
Northern India, early 18th century
Los Angeles County Museum of Art
(From the Nasli and Alice Heeramaneck
Collection, Museum Associates Purchase),
M.76.2.13
PAGE 222

46 Huqqa base with floral design
Glass with painted flowers, etched and
painted in royal blue and gold
11.2 cm high
Rajasthan, 18th century
Varanasi, Bharat Kala Bhavan, 3/9102
PAGE 223

50 Jewel turban ornament (kalgi)
Gold set with rubies, diamonds and
emeralds
17 cm high, 6 cm wide
Northern India, 18th century
London, Victoria and Albert Museum,
IM 240-1923
PAGE 229

51 Turban ornament (sarpech)
Enamelled gold with diamonds and
emeralds
12 cm high, 16 cm wide
Lahore, 19th century
Paris, Musée Guimet, Musée National des
Arts Asiatiques, MA 6762
PAGE 228

52 Necklace
Gold with enamel
14 cm
Udaipur, 19th century
New Delhi, National Museum, 96.233
PAGE 227

53 Navratna necklace
Gold with champlevé-enamelled back
16 cm
Jaipur, 18th century
New Delhi, National Museum, 64.142
PAGE 253 (TOP)

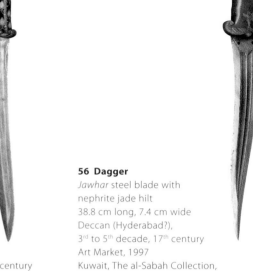

JADE

54 Dagger
Steel blade with nephrite
jade hilt inlaid with gold
in *kundan* technique, set
with rubies, emeralds and
diamonds
35.4 cm long, 8 cm wide
Northern India or Deccan, mid-17th century
Art Market, 1980s
Kuwait, The al-Sabah Collection,
Dar al-Athar al-Islamiyyah, LNS 12 HS
PAGE 220

55 Dagger
Jawhar steel blade, hilt
from nephrite jade inlaid
with gold in *kundan*
technique, set with
nephrite jade and rubies
39 cm long, 10 cm wide
Deccan (?), second quarter, 17th century
Art Market, 1980s
Kuwait, The al-Sabah Collection,
Dar al-Athar al-Islamiyyah, LNS 115 J
PAGE 220

56 Dagger
Jawhar steel blade with
nephrite jade hilt
38.8 cm long, 7.4 cm wide
Deccan (Hyderabad?),
3rd to 5th decade, 17th century
Art Market, 1997
Kuwait, The al-Sabah Collection,
Dar al-Athar al-Islamiyyah, LNS 264 HS
PAGE 221

61 Dagger hilt in the form of a horse head
Carved jade
14.1 cm high
Delhi, early 17th century
Mumbai, Chhatrapati Shivaji Maharaj Vastu
Sangrahalaya, 15.122
PAGE 255

62 Leaf-shaped tray
Carved white jade
12.8 cm long, 10.6 cm broad
Deccan(?), 17th century
Hyderabad, Salar Jung Museum,
216/XLIX
PAGE 215

63 Wine cup of Shah Jahan
White nephrite jade
14 cm high, 18.7 cm wide
Northern India, dated 1657
London, Victoria and Albert Museum,
IS.12-1962
PAGE 216

57 Dagger
Jawhar steel blade, hilt from
nephrite jade inlaid with gold
in *kundan* technique, set with
a ruby and diamonds at a
later date
39.5 cm long, 8.4 cm wide
Deccan (Hyderabad?), 1st third,
17th century
Art Market, 1991
Kuwait, The al-Sabah Collection,
Dar al-Athar al-Islamiyyah, LNS 80 HS
PAGE 221

58 Dagger (khanjar)
Steel blade with jade hilt
inset with rubies
35.8 cm long
Northern India,
18th century
Paris, Musée Guimet, Musée National des
Arts Asiatiques,
MA 6797
PAGE 254

**59 Dagger with hilt in the
form of a ram head**
Steel blade with light green
jade hilt
35.5 cm long
Northern India,
late 17th century
Mumbai, Chhatrapati Shivaji Maharaj Vastu
Sangrahalaya (Sir Ratan Tata Collection)
22.3850
PAGE 254

**60 Dagger with hilt in
the form of a nilgai**
Nephrite and steel
38.1 cm long
Northern India,
17th century
New York, The Metropolitan Museum of
Art (Gift of Alice Heeramaneck, in memory
of Nasli Heeramaneck, 1985), 1985.58a
PAGE 255

64 Bowl with lotus design
Carved white jade
3.4 cm high, 14.8 cm diameter
Northern India, late 17th century
Mumbai, Chhatrapati Shivaji Maharaj Vastu
Sangrahalaya (Sir Ratan Tata Collection),
22.1329
PAGE 217

65 Huqqa bowl with trellis design
White jade inlaid with lapis lazuli, green
jade and gold
18 cm high, 17 cm diameter
Northern India, beginning 18th century
Private Collection
PAGES 60—61

66 Trinket box with arabesque design
Green jade with gold inserts
16.8 cm long, 9.6 cm broad
Deccan, 17th century
Hyderabad, Salar Jung Museum,
211/XLIX
PAGE 129

JADE

67 Upper armband (bazuband) centrepiece
Nephrite jade, inlaid with gold and set in *kundan* technique with a synthetic ruby cabochon, with gold champlevé-enamelled bails
7 cm long, 4 cm diameter (rosette), 1.4 cm thick
Northern India or Deccan, late 16ᵗʰ-early 17ᵗʰ century (ruby and setting modern)
Art Market, 1994
Kuwait, The al-Sabah Collection, Dar al-Athar al-Islamiyyah, LNS 1132 J
PAGE 214

68 Mirror-back with trellis design
Jade with gold and white jade inserts
13 cm long, 11 cm wide
Northern India, 18ᵗʰ century
London, Victoria and Albert Museum, IS.02587
PAGE 101

69 Mirror-back with perforated floral design
Pale green jade inset with precious stones
23.7 cm high, 21 cm wide
Delhi, early 19ᵗʰ century
Oxford, Ashmolean Museum, EA X.2327
PAGE 175

IVORY

71 Panel with flowering plants
Carved ivory
8.8 cm high, 23.8 cm wide
Northern India, 17ᵗʰ century
Paris, Musée Guimet, Musée National des Arts Asiatiques, MA 6816
PAGE 162

72 Powder priming flask
Polychromed ivory, garnets, rubies, and steel
19.6 cm long, 7.6 cm wide, 3.1 cm deep
Northern India, mid-17ᵗʰ century
Richmond, Virginia Museum of Fine Arts (The Nasli and Alice Heeramaneck Collection, Gift of Paul Mellon), 68.8.142
PAGE 256

73 Powder priming flask
Ivory carved in relief with deer, lions, and other animals
31.5 cm long
Northern India, 17ᵗʰ century
Paris, Musée Guimet, Musée National des Arts Asiatiques, MA 6818
PAGE 257

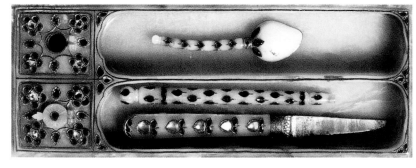

70 Writing set
Nephrite jade embellished with diamonds,
rubies, and emeralds set in gold
20.5 cm long, 8.8 cm wide
Northern India, *ca.* 1700
London, Victoria and Albert Museum,
IS.02549
PAGES 218—219

COINS

74 Mohur of Jahangir
Struck gold
2.5 cm diameter
Mint of Agra, dated 1608
London, British Museum, BMC 295,
1888.12.8.739
PAGE 152

75 Mohur of Jahangir
Struck gold
3.7 cm diameter
Mint of Agra, dated 1619
London, British Museum, BMC 305,
IOC 1909
PAGE 152

METALWORK

76 Vase with calligraphy
Brass, engraved and inlaid with black lac
12.3 cm high, 15.4 cm diameter
Lahore, *ca.* 1580-1600
London, Victoria and Albert Museum,
IS.21-1889
PAGE 150

77 Bowl with hunting scene and inscription
Copper, engraved and polished
15.5 cm high, 34.5 cm diameter
Northern India, dated 1582
Mumbai, Chhatrapati Shivaji Maharaj Vastu
Sangrahalaya, 56.61
PAGES 260—261

78 Beaker and cover with floral design
Silver, chased and engraved
14.2 cm high, 8.3 cm diameter
Northern India, mid-17th century
London, Victoria and Albert Museum,
IS.31-1961
PAGE 41

83 Plate with petalled design
Alloy inlaid with brass and silver (*bidri*)
3.5 cm high, 31 cm diameter
Deccan, late 17th century
Copenhagen, The David Collection,
16/1987
PAGE 98

84 Plate with chevron design
Alloy inlaid with brass and silver (*bidri*)
32.8 cm diameter
Bidar, Deccan, 19th century
Hyderabad, Salar Jung Museum,
268/1, XXXIII (56.384)
PAGE 99

85 Plate with calligraphy
Copper
26 cm diameter
Northern India, 18th century
New Delhi, National Museum, 62.111
PAGE 151

79 Ewer with arabesque design
Alloy inlaid with brass and silver (*bidri*)
28.5 cm high
Bidar, Deccan, 17th century
London, Victoria and Albert Museum,
1479-1904
PAGE 128

80 Powder box with floral design
Alloy Inlaid with brass and silver (*bidri*)
13.1 cm dlameter
Bidar, Deccan, 19th century
Hyderabad, Salar Jung Museum,
258/XXXIII (56.242)
PAGE 232

81 Huqqa base with floral design
Alloy Inlaid with brass and silver (*bidri*)
18.6 cm high, 16.8 cm diameter
BIdar, Deccan, late 17th century
London, Victoria and Albert Museum,
IS.27-1980
PAGE 233

82 Tray with floral motif
Alloy inlaid with brass and silver (*bidri*)
33.4 cm diameter
Bidar, Deccan, 17th century
Richmond, Virginia Museum of Fine Arts
(The Arthur and Margaret Glasgow Fund),
86.196
PAGES 234—235

86 Circular basin with perforated cover
Alloy inlaid with silver (*bidri*)
14.3 cm high, 42.6 cm diameter
Bidar, Deccan, 17th century
Hyderabad, Salar Jung Museum,
268/1, XXXIII (56.181)
PAGE 96

87 Octagonal tray with floral motifs
Gold with red, green, and white
enamel, emeralds and rubies
30.8 cm diameter
Northern India, 17th century
St Petersburg, The State Hermitage
Museum, V3-724
PAGE 224

88 Plate with floral motifs
Gold with red, green, and white enamel
19.7 cm diameter
Northern India, 17th century
St Petersburg, The State Hermitage
Museum, V3-716
PAGE 225

89 Plate with floral motifs
Gold with red, green and white enamel
19 cm diameter
Northern India, 17th century
St Petersburg, The State Hermitage
Museum, V3-705
PAGES 58—59

METALWORK

90 Pandan box with cover and tray decorated with flowers
Gold with red, green and white enamel
Box: 9.8 cm high; 13.2 cm diameter
Tray: 31.2 cm diameter
Northern India, *ca.* 1700
London, Nasser D. Khalili Collection of Islamic Art, JLY 1720.
PAGE 226

91 Box with a panel of birds
Gold-enamelled in champlevé technique
4 cm high, 4.2 cm long, 3 cm wide
Deccan, 18th century
New Delhi, National Museum, 94.89
PAGE 253 (BOTTOM)

92 Huqqa base with animals and birds
Silver gilt with multi-coloured enamels
20 cm high, 22 cm diameter at base
Northern India, late 18th century
Private Collection
PAGE 251

ARMS & ARMOUR

94 Dagger
Steel blade, hilt gold over iron core, champlevé-enamelled, set in *kundan* technique, with diamonds and rubies
37 cm long, 8.1 cm wide
Probably Hyderabad, 18th century
Art Market, 1980s
Kuwait, The al-Sabah Collection, Dar al-Athar al-Islamiyyah, LNS 26 Ja
PAGE 220

95 Sword of Tipu Sultan, with standard hilt and a broad embellished blade
Steel
74.1 cm long
Srirangapatnam, Mysore, *ca.* 1790
New Delhi, National Museum, 56.17/1
PAGES 148—149

96 Sword hilt
Steel, inlaid with gold
16 cm long; 8.1 cm wide; 5.9 cm diameter
Deccan (Hyderabad ?)
17th century
Kuwait, The al-Sabah Collection
Dar al-Athar al-Islamiyyah, LNS 295 M
PAGE 230

93 Lota: covered jar on narrow foot
Cloisonné enamel on gold
14.4 cm high, 10.2 cm diameter
Jaipur, late 17th/early 18th century
Cleveland Museum of Art (Purchase from
the J.H. Wade Fund), 1962.206
PAGE 100

97 Sword hilt
Steel, overlaid with gold
16.2 cm long; 8.1 cm wide; 5.9 cm
diameter
Deccan (Hyderabad ?), 2nd-3rd quarter
17th century
Kuwait, The al-Sabah Collection
Dar al-Athar al-Islamiyyah, LNS 297 M
PAGE 231

**98 Body-guard ornamented with
arabesque design**
Steel, border damascened in gold
30 cm high, 23 cm wide
Hyderabad, 18th century
Hyderabad, Salar Jung Museum,
203/LIVA
PAGE 130

**99 Arm guard (bazuband) with
arabesque motifs**
Steel
33.5 cm high, 10 cm wide
Northern India, 17th century
New Delhi, National Museum, 62.2318/2.3
PAGE 131

100 Bow of Bahadur Shah Zafar II
Steel, damascened in gold
104 cm long
Delhi, *ca.* 1848
New Delhi, National Museum, 59.2
PAGES 148—149

Key monuments

DELHI

AURANGABAD

FATEHPUR SIKRI

RED FORT

Built in 1639—48 as the principal residence of Shah Jahan, the Red Fort on the Yamuna River in Delhi formed the architectural focus of the new city, named Shahjahanabad after its imperial founder. The fort is contained within a rectangle of massive stone walls, entered in the middle of the western side through a monumental gateway that gives access to a covered bazaar. This leads directly to the Diwan-i Amm where Shah Jahan held formal audience on a daily basis. To the rear, overlooking the Yamuna, are the private pavilions and apartments. These are aligned in a row, linked by a marble water channel with fountains, opening onto walled pleasure gardens. The Moti Masjid was added by Aurangzeb in 1663 (see endpapers and pp. 4—5, 105, 106—107, 119 & 280).

BIBI-KA MAQBARA

The tomb of Aurangzeb's wife Rabia Daurani, known as Bibi-ka Maqbara, is located in a garden complex outside Aurangabad where Aurangzeb spent the last years of his reign fighting to maintain Mughal control of the Deccan. Built by the emperor in 1661 in obvious imitation of the Taj Mahal, the Bibi-ka Maqbara also has a quartet of slender minarets framing the central domed mausoleum. This has symmetrically disposed arched portals facing the four directions; its proportions, however, are much more slender. The octagonal chamber has a gallery with a view of the tomb below; there is no upper cenotaph as in the Taj. Instead of the white marble of the Taj, the tomb employs finely executed plasterwork (see p. 288).

PALACE COMPLEX

Built in 1571—85 by Akbar in fulfillment of a vow to Shaykh Salim Chishti, the Sufi saint who had predicted the birth of a son, this imperial city located 40 kilometres west of Agra served as Akbar's principal residence during the 1580s. The ensemble of royal buildings stands on a ridge, approached along a bazaar street. The palace itself is divided into a sequence of walled courtyards, in the middle of which stand red sandstone buildings of imaginative designs, used by Akbar and his courtiers for both everyday business and pleasurable diversions. A sophisticated hydraulic system provided water for ornamental pools and *hammams*. Kitchens, stables, caravanserais, workshops and stores are all located nearby (see pp. 20—21, 50—51 & 168—169).

JAMI MOSQUE & TOMB OF SHAYKH SALIM CHISHTI

A short distance from the palace at Fatehpur Sikri stands the Jami Mosque built in 1575. It is entered from the south through a lofty arched gateway, the Buland Darwaza, reached by a steep flight of steps. The prayer hall at the western end of the mosque's spacious courtyard has a sequence of five chambers roofed by alternating domes and vaults. Standing freely on the northern side of the courtyard is the white marble tomb of Shaykh Salim Chishti, built by Akbar after the saint's death in 1581. It is surrounded by finely worked geometric *jalis* of different designs, shielded by an angled overhang carried on cut-out, serpentine brackets. The screens admit light to the corridor that surrounds the domed chamber where the saint is entombed beneath a wooden canopy (see pp. 134—135 & 140—141).

The Rang Mahal in the Red Fort in Delhi has a lotus fountain with twenty-four radial petals sculpted directly out of the white marble floor. The fountain was fed by an open water channel that linked the various pavilions used by Shah Jahan and his nobles. Precious stones were once inset into the engraved designs that surround the fountain.

AGRA

RED FORT

The pre-Mughal period citadel on the right bank of the Yamuna River at Agra was used by Babur as his headquarters, but it was Akbar who in 1564—70 had the earlier mud brick walls replaced by massive red sandstone ramparts. Laid out in a semicircle facing the river, the fort is entered from the west through an imposing gateway that leads to a long bazaar street. Of Akbar's addition within the walls, only the so-called Jahangiri Mahal, a private residence, still stands. In 1628—37 Shah Jahan made substantial additions, adding the Diwan-i Amm for public audience, which faced onto a vast square, as well as the Diwan-i Khass for private meetings, and the Khass Mahal and other pavilions overlooking the river for personal use (see pp. 142—143).

TOMB OF AKBAR

When Akbar died in 1605, his tomb at Sikandra outside Agra remained unfinished, and in 1613 his son and successor Jahangir completed the project. The mausoleum stands in the middle of a vast *char-bagh* garden with axial waterways, entered on the south through a gateway with bold polychrome designs. The emperor's tomb is located within a domed chamber at ground level, above which rises a multi-storey structure with open pavilion-like *chhatris* arranged at different levels in pyramidal formation; there is no dome. Possibly, the whole structure was intended to be topped by a *chhatri*, but Jahangir added a terrace encased by marble screens, in the middle of which is Akbar's cenotaph, open to the sky (see pp. 34, 73, 74—75, 116, 126—127, 132—133, 166—167 & 188—189).

TOMB OF ITIMAD-AD DAULA

Standing in a walled garden with axial waterways on the left bank of the Yamuna, the tomb of Itimad-ad Daula was built by Jahangir's wife Nur Jahan for her father in 1626-28. The mausoleum is an exquisitely finished, perfectly symmetrical structure built entirely of white marble. A domed chamber at ground level houses the tomb itself, above which at rooftop level is a vaulted pavilion encased in *jali* screens. Octagonal towers with domical pavilions mark the four corners. The geometric and arabesque patterns in polychrome stonework and the painted floral designs are among the finest in all Mughal architecture. Gateways are positioned in the middle of each side of the garden; that on the west gives access to the river (see pp. 54—55, 76—77, 79—86, 94—95, 112—115, 117, 182—183 & 186—187).

TAJ MAHAL

World renowned as the tomb of Shah Jahan's beloved wife, Mumtaz Mahal, the Taj Mahal was built in 1632—43 by the emperor, and it was here that he himself was buried in 1658. The tomb is elevated on a terrace overlooking the Yamuna at the northern end of a *char-bagh* garden with axial water channels and fountains. The tomb is faced entirely in white marble, relieved by delicate *pietra dura* inlays and relief panels. The design is strictly symmetrical and perfectly proportioned: lofty arched portals facing the four directions are flanked by double tiers of lesser arched recesses; the whole composition is topped by a slightly bulbous dome no less than 56 metres high above the terrace. The composition is balanced by detached circular minarets at the four corners. The white marble tomb and minarets are flanked by a red sandstone mosque and identical matching structure at either end of the terrace (see Title page, Contents page and pp. 6—7, 52—53, 72, 97, 118, 120—121, 144—145, 160—161, 170—174 & 176—181).

LAHORE

FORT

In the late 1580s Akbar shifted his principal headquarters to Lahore, constructing a highly fortified palace on the edge of the city overlooking the Ravi River, with a Diwan-i Amm facing onto a large rectangular courtyard. The fort was substantially remodelled in 1617—20 by Jahangir, who completed Akbar's colonnaded quadrangle by adding reception halls to the rear of the Diwan-i Amm, as well as several residential pavilions with private courtyards and gardens. The splendid coloured tiled panels adorning the outer walls of the riverside and west fronts of the fort date from his period. However, it was Aurangzeb who built the massive Alamgiri gate in 1674 that serves as the main entrance to the fort from the west (see pp. 88—89, 122—123 & 236—237).

BADSHAHI MOSQUE

With a courtyard measuring no less than 175 metres square, Aurangzeb's Badshahi Mosque of 1674 is the largest place of prayer to be built during the Mughal era. It stands immediately opposite the Alamgiri gate of the fort, and is itself entered through an imposing arched portal. Lofty tapering octagonal minarets topped by domed pavilions mark the four corners of the courtyard. The prayer hall has a trio of white marble domes, the central one rising slightly higher over the principal entrance. Vaulted corridors and chambers linking the three domed chambers within are adorned with fine painted and relief plaster decoration. The traditional ablution tank is situated in the middle of the entrance courtyard (see pp. 92—93, 102—103 & 204—205).

WAZIR KHAN'S MOSQUE

Hidden away in the streets of the walled city of Lahore, this mosque was erected in 1634 by Wazir Khan, the Mughal governor of Punjab under Shah Jahan. It is of interest for its splendid coloured tile mosaics, the finest of any Mughal mosque. The tiles pervade the whole structure — they almost entirely cover the entrance portal, the internal walls of the rectangular courtyard, the angled sides of the octagonal minarets that rise from its four corners, and the facade of the prayer hall itself. Calligraphic panels quoting religious texts alternate with fanciful compositions with flowers in vases and cypresses. Similar themes decorate the domed interior of the prayer hall, but these are realized in painted plaster rather than coloured tilework (see pp. 146—147 & 184—185)

TOMBS OF JAHANGIR, NUR JAHAN & ASAF KHAN

Located at Shahdara, a short distance outside Lahore, the mausoleum of Jahangir was built in the middle of a *char-bagh* garden by Shah Jahan in 1628—38. This simple structure has a tomb accommodated in a domed chamber set at the core of an arcaded podium. The corners of the podium are marked by octagonal, four-stage minarets, topped by open pavilions. The rooftop terrace is devoid of any surmounting chamber, but the arcades beneath are enlivened with coloured tile mosaics, while delicate stone inlays decorate the tomb itself. The mausoleums of Jahangir's favourite queen Nur Jahan and her brother Asaf Khan, who died in 1645 and 1641 respectively, are located in the adjacent gardens (see pp. 87 & 90—91).

GLOSSARY

Akbar Nama: biography of Akbar authored by his friend and adviser Abu'l Fazl

bangla: pavilion with curved ridge and cornice, derived from Bengal

bazuband: arm-guard of metal, also upper-arm ornament

bidri: technique of inlaying metalwork composed of a dark zinc alloy with silver and brass; named after Bidar, a town in the Deccan

buta: stylized flowering plant motif on Kashmiri textiles

char-bagh: four-square garden of Persian origin favoured by the Mughals for their palaces and tombs

chhatri: domed and pillared pavilion, often crowning a tower or minaret

chikan: type of cotton embroidery, most often white on white

Chishti: Sufi sect to which many of the saints patronized by the Mughals belonged

cuerda seca: technique of firing tiles with multiple coloured designs

Diwan-i Amm: hall of public audience in a Mughal palace

Diwan-i Khass: hall of private audience in a Mughal palace

huqqa bowl: glass, jade or metal bowl to hold the pipes with which tobacco was smoked

jali: perforated screen, generally of stone, to filter the outdoor light

jamdani: intricate loom-embroidered weaving method

kalamkari: technique of dyeing, printing and painting cotton cloths

kalgi: jewelled turban ornament

Kalima: Profession of Faith: There is no god but God, and Muhammad is his Prophet

kanat: tent panel

karkhana: imperial workshop producing textiles, carpets, metalware, and other fine arts

khilat: robe of honour

kitabkhana: imperial library and accompanying workshop employing calligraphers, illuminators and painters

kundan: jewellers' technique of setting precious stones into gold

Lal Qila: Red Fort, as in Agra and Delhi

mahal: hall of a palace

malmal: muslin cloth

mihrab: prayer niche in a mosque facing towards Mecca

mohur: gold coin of different values issued by the Mughal emperors

naskh: style of Persian calligraphy

nasta`liq: style of Persian calligraphy widely used in Mughal manuscripts

nilgai: type of Indian deer

pandan: box for storing *pan,* areca nut and betel leaf offered after a meal

patka: waist-sash

pietra dura: from *commesso di pietra dura,* an Italian technique imported into India of setting different coloured, semiprecious stones into a marble base

qalib kari: mouldwork

qit'a: display page to demonstrate calligrapher's skill

Shaykh: formal title of a saint

sarpech: jewelled turban ornament

shamsa: decorative sunburst rosette on an illuminated page

sherwani: fitted knee-length man's formal coat

shish mahal: mirror hall, usually with mirror pieces set into the ceiling and walls

simurgh: fantastic bird of Chinese origin, introduced to India via Persian art

Sura: chapter of the Koran

svastika: swastika, Indian motif in the shape of a cross, rotating clockwise

thuluth: style of calligraphy preferred for Koranic inscriptions in Mughal architecture

tughra: decorative calligraphic signature

CHRONOLOGY OF MUGHAL EMPERORS

BABUR, ruled 1526—30

HUMAYUN, ruled 1530—40; in exile 1540—55; ruled again in India 1555—56

AKBAR, ruled 1556—1605

JAHANGIR, Prince Salim, ruled 1605—27

SHAH JAHAN, Prince Khurram, ruled 1628—58; died in confinement in 1666

AURANGZEB, ALAMGIR I, ruled 1658—1707

SHAH ALAM, BAHADUR SHAH I, ruled 1707—12

FARRUKHSIYAR, ruled 1713—19

MUHAMMAD SHAH, ruled 1719—48

AHMAD SHAH, ruled 1748—54

ALAMGIR II, ruled 1754—59

SHAH ALAM II, ruled 1759—1806

AKBAR SHAH II, ruled 1806—37

BAHADUR SHAH ZAFAR II, ruled 1837—58; died in exile 1862

Select bibliography

HISTORY

Eraly, Abraham, *Emperors of the Peacock Throne: The Saga of the Great Mughals*, New Delhi, 1997

Gascoigne, Bamber, *The Great Moghals*, London, 1971

Hambly, Gavin, *Cities of Mughal India: Delhi, Agra and Fatehpur Sikri*, New York, 1968

Mikhia, Harbans, *The Mughals of India*, Oxford, 2004

Richards, John F, *The Mughal Empire*, Cambridge, 1993

ARCHITECTURE

Alfieri, Bianca Maria, *Islamic Architecture of the Indian Subcontinent*, London, 2000

Asher, Catherine B, *Architecture of Mughal India*, Cambridge, 1992

Begley, W E, *Monumental Islamic Calligraphy from India*, Villa Park, Illinois, 1985

—, 'Amanat Khan and the Calligraphy on the Taj Mahal,' *Kunst des Orients*, 12 (1978—79), pp. 5—60

Chaghatai, M Abdullah, *The Wazir Khan Mosque, Lahore: History and Architecture*, Lahore, 1975

Crowe, Sylvia, Sheila Haywood and Susan Jellicoe, *The Gardens of Mughal India*, London, 1972

Koch, Ebba, *Mughal Architecture*, Munich, 1991

—, *Mughal Art and Imperial Ideology*, New Delhi, 2001

—, *The Complete Taj Mahal and the Riverfront Gardens of Agra*, London, 2006

Latif, S Muhammad, *Lahore: Architectural Remains*, reprinted, Lahore, 1981

Nath, R, *Colour Decoration in Mughal Architecture*, Bombay, 1970

—, *History of Decorative Art in Mughal Architecture*, Delhi and Varanasi, 1976

Nicholson, Louise, *The Red Fort, Delhi*, London, 1989

Okada, Amina and Jean-Louis Nou, *Taj Mahal*, Paris, 1998

—, *A Jewel of Mughal India: The Tomb of Itimad ud-Daulah*, Milan, 2003

Siddiqi, W H, *Fatehpur Sikri*, New Delhi, 1972

Smith, Edmund W, *The Moghul Architecture of Fatehpur Sikri*, 4 volumes, reprinted, Delhi, 1985

Vogel, J P, *Tile-Mosaics of the Lahore Fort*, Calcutta, 1920

Wheeler, Mortimer, editor, *Splendours of the East: Temples, Tombs, Palaces and Fortresses of Asia*, London, 1965

FINE ARTS

Brand, Michael and Glen D Lowry, *Akbar's India: Art from the Mughal City of Victory*, Asia Society, New York, 1985

Crill, Rosemary, Susan Stronge and Andrew Topsfield, editors, *Arts of Mughal India: Studies in Honour of Robert Skelton*, London, 2004

Desai, Vishakha, *Life at Court: Art for India's Rulers, 16th-19th Centuries*, Museum of Fine Arts, Boston, 1985

Harle, J C and Andrew Topsfield, *Indian Art in the Ashmolean Museum*, Oxford, 1987

Jones, Dalu, editor, *A Mirror of Princes: The Mughals and the Medici*, Bombay, 1987

Khandalawala, Karl, editor, *An Age of Splendour: Islamic Art in India*, Bombay, 1983

Pal, Pratapaditya, et al, *Romance of the Taj Mahal*, Los Angeles County Museum of Art, Los Angeles, 1989

Skelton, Robert et al, *The Indian Heritage: Court Life & Arts under Mughal Rule*, Victoria and Albert Museum, London, 1982

Smart, Ellen S and Daniel S Walker, *Pride of the Princes: Indian Art of the Mughal Era in the Cincinnati Art Museum*, Cincinnati, 1985

Verma, Som Prakash, *Flora and Fauna in Mughal Art*, Mumbai, 1999

Welch, Stuart Cary, *The Art of Mughal India*, Asia Society, New York, 1963

—, *India: Art and Culture, 1300—1900*, The Metropolitan Museum of Art, New York, 1985

Zebrowski, Mark, 'Decorative Arts of the Mughal Period,' in Basil Gray, editor, *The Arts of India*, pp. 177—189, Oxford, 1981

MINIATURE PAINTING

Beach, Milo Cleveland, *The Grand Mogul: Imperial Painting in India (1600—1660)*, Williamstown, Mass., 1978

—, *The Imperial Image: Paintings for the Mughal Court*, Freer Gallery of Art, Washington, 1981

Blair, Sheila S, *Islamic Calligraphy*, Chapter 12, Edinburgh, 2006

Daljeet, *Mughal and Deccani Paintings from the Collection of the National Museum*, New Delhi, 1999

Okada, Amina, *Indian Miniatures of the Mughal Court*, New York, 1992

Pal, Pratapaditya, editor, *Master Artists of the Imperial Mughal Court*, Bombay, 1991

Rogers, J M, *Mughal Miniatures*, London, 1993

Stronge, Susan, *Painting for the Mughal Emperor: The Art of the Book, 1560—1660*, London, 2002

Verma, Som Prakash, *Painting, the Mughal Experience*, New Delhi, 2005

JEWELRY, METALWORK, ARMS AND COINS

Balakrishnan, Usha R and Meera Sushil Kumar, *Dance of the Peacock*, Mumbai, 1999

Haider, Syed Zafar, *Islamic Arms and Armour of Muslim India*, Lahore, 1991

Keene, Manuel with Salam Kaoukji, *Treasury of the World, Jeweled Arts of India in the Age of the Mughals: The Al-Sabah Collection, Kuwait National Museum*, London, 2001

Kulkarni, Prashant P, 'Where Art Meets Wealth: Mughal Coins,' In Martha L Carter, editor, *A Treasury of Indian Coins*, pp. 89—104, Bombay, 1994

Markel, Stephen, 'Inception and Maturation in Mughal Jades,' *Marg*, XLIV/2 (1992), pp. 49—64

Pant, G N, *Catalogue of Edged Arms and Armour in Salar Jung Museum*, Hyderabad, 1989

Paul, E Jaiwant, *Arms and Armour: Traditional Weapons of India*, New Delhi, 2005

Poole, Stanley Lane, *The Coins of the Moghul Emperors of Hindustan in the British Museum*, London, 1892

Sharma, Rita Devi and M Varadarajan, *Handcrafted Indian Enamel Jewelery*, New Delhi, 2004

Stronge, Susan, *Bidriware*, London, 1985

Stronge, Susan, Nina Smith and J C Harle, *A Golden Treasury: Jewelery from the Indian Subcontinent*, Victoria and Albert Museum, London, 1988

Zebrowski, Mark, *Gold, Silver & Bronze from Mughal India*, London, 1997

CARPETS AND TEXTILES

Agrawal, Yashodhara, *Silk Brocades*, New Delhi, 2003

Barnes, Ruth, Steven Cohen and Rosemary Crill, *Trade, Temple and Court: Indian Textiles from the Tapi Collection*, Mumbai, 2003

Irwin, John and Margaret Hall, *Indian Printed and Painted Fabrics*, Calico Museum, Ahmedabad, 1971

—, *Indian Embroideries*, Calico Museum, Ahmedabad, 1973

Levi-Strauss, Monique, *The Romance of the Cashmere Shawl*, Milan and Ahmedabad, 1986

Mathur, Asha Rani, *Indian Shawls: Mantles of Splendour*, New Delhi, 2004

Walker, Daniel, *Flowers Underfoot: Indian Carpets of the Mughal Period*, Metropolitan Museum of Art, New York, 1998

Acknowledgments

Without the generous counsel of a number of friends and colleagues it is unlikely that the author would ever have dared to embark upon this volume. Tristram Holland helped in the initial stages of formulating the overall concept; Mumtaz Currim acted as a general researcher, advising on objects in Indian collections to be included, and checking details of Mughal history, architecture and art; Carmen Kagal offered invaluable suggestions for improving the text.

Throughout, the author benefited from the specialized knowledge of a number of individuals: Dalu Jones has been a source of inspiration on all aspects of Islamic art; John Robert Alderman shared his vast experience of Indian decorative arts; Bruce Wannell categorized the different calligraphic scripts and traced the textual quotations; Gita Wagle detected the individual stones used in Mughal *pietra dura* decoration; meetings with Ebba Koch, the pre-eminent scholar of Mughal architecture and related arts, proved informative and stimulating. Rosemary Crill of the Victoria and Albert Museum, London, and Helen Philon, formerly of the Benaki Museum, Athens, have been particularly helpful.

Architectural details of the Mughal monuments reproduced here have been captured with striking realism in the splendid images of Malcolm Hutcheson, Antonio Martinelli, Amit Pasricha and Bharath Ramamrutham, and those of the late Jean-Louis Nou and Mark Zebrowski. Permission to reproduce photographs of monuments in Delhi, Agra and Fatehpur Sikri has graciously been granted by the Director General, Archaeological Survey of India. Photographs of manuscripts and paintings, carpets and textiles, jades and ivories, and metalwares are mostly provided by the relevant museums.

At the IBH office in Mumbai the author greatly enjoyed working with Nidhi Sah on the layouts, while Pooja Vir, Biswajeet Rath and Neeyati Shethia commissioned the photographs, sought out details of the objects to be included in the Catalogue, and generally oversaw progress of the project. Without the warmhearted and constant encouragement of Meera Ahuja and Padmini Mirchandani the volume would never have taken off, let alone been completed.

To all these individuals and institutions the author offers his grateful thanks. As on so many other occasions, John M. Fritz provided the author with unstinting personal support.

GEORGE MICHELL

PHOTO CREDITS

FOLLOWING PAGE This brass panel with an embossed design of an iris flower with three blooms set within an arched frame adorns a wooden door of the Bibi-ka Maqbara in Aurangabad. The composition is virtually identical to that found in printed cotton and velvet hangings (*see* pp. 192—193). The naturalism of the flower, however, recalls the finest relief stone carving and miniature painting of the period.